The Study Skills Curriculum
Developing Organized Successful Students
Elementary – High School

Downloadable Forms
Easy to Implement Lessons Using Strategies from
"Learning the ROPES for Improved Executive Function"

Patricia Schetter, M.A., B.C.B.A.

Victoria Murphy, M.S., B.C.B.A.

Autism and Behavior Training Associates
*"Helping you find the keys to
unlock the potential of students
on the Autism Spectrum"*

ABTA Publications
Redding, CA USA

Autism & Behavior Training Associates
ABTA Publications and Products
PO Box 492123
Redding, CA 96049

For information on ordering this manual or on workshops provided by Autism & Behavior Training Associates on this and other topics, please see our websites at:

www.autismandbehavior.com

www.abtaproducts.com

Learning the ROPES Study Skills Curriculum for Improved Executive Function

ISBN 978-0-9844660-6-1
Copyright © 2017 Autism & Behavior Training Associates,
    Patricia Schetter, M.A., B.C.B.A.,
    Victoria Murphy, M.S., B.C.B.A.
    All rights reserved

Cover design and photo by Mary A Livingston

Introduction

Executive Functions (EF) are the cognitive processes thought to be responsible for many of our organizational and problem-solving skills and abilities. These are the planning processes that we automatically use at the beginning of a task and when dealing with novel situations. They are the "ability to maintain an appropriate problem solving set for the attainment of a future goal" (Welsh, M., and Pennington, B., 1988).

While EF is considered to be a cognitive capacity, much like a person's IQ, anyone can learn skills and strategies to improve their organizational and problem solving skills. Many students who have the intellectual capacity to be excellent students begin to fail in school due to an inability to plan, organize, and complete the increasingly complex assignments given. In addition, an inability to prioritize and keep track of the social, functional, and extracurricular demands becomes quite overwhelming starting in late elementary school and peaking in high school, when grades and academic performance become high stakes.

As these students struggle and recognize their lack of success, many begin to experience anxiety and depression. Some may drop out of school, turn to drugs or alcohol, or begin a relationship with the judicial system. As a result of frustration, many students act out to protest the demands that they cannot properly organize or understand. Frequently, these students are referred to special education or are the students identified as "behavior problems" and are well known by campus security and office administration.

The focus for the students that we just described is typically on decreasing all of the "maladaptive behaviors," usually through discipline and punitive consequences, but little is done to teach them the skills that will eventually end their frustrations and lead to their independence and success. In order to support these students, educators must first recognize that their behavior problems may be the direct result of underlying learning differences or skill deficits in the area of Executive Functioning. They are not simply due to insufficient motivation. The acting out or shutting down behaviors may be a mask for a real issue that, unless addressed, may result in many lifelong struggles.

This Study Skills Curriculum was developed based on an identified need expressed by Resource Specialists and intervention teachers who work directly with these students. Many of the specialists offered "Study Skills" classes beginning in middle and high school. These classes are intended to provide support with work completion. However, it has been our experience that often these "Study Skills" classes are really more like a study hall where students are expected to initiate work completion and make good use of their time. In these classes, little instruction on strategies for better organizational skills is provided and many times it simply becomes another class period in which the student acts out.

All of the lessons in this curriculum were derived from the concepts found in the book Learning the ROPES for Improved Executive Functioning Skills (Schetter 2003). Although reading this book is helpful in implementing this curriculum it is not a requirement. This curriculum includes everything a teacher needs to complete the lessons and activities to teach students the skills to improve their executive functions.

The purpose of the Study Skills Curriculum is to systematically teach students how to become better organized, thus more successful in school and as adults. Each unit begins with an objective(s) and "Content for Teachers". This information is followed by lessons which are broken down into activities to build students' executive functioning skills.

The Study Skills Curriculum was designed to be completed across a school year. The frequency and duration of the activities should be based on students needs and the structure and design of the program in which it is being implemented within. The various activities may be completed daily or across several days.

This Study Skills Curriculum has been an effective tool for use in specific study skill classes. However, these lessons may be used by any person who is attempting to improve executive functioning skills in others. It is essential that the concepts from the lessons be incorporated across assignments from various classes and life situations so that the students can see how the strategies apply to their real lives.

The Scope and Sequence section of this curriculum will provide an overview of all the lessons and activities. A year long program may be developed based on the Scope and Sequence of the Study Skills Curriculum. Longer units may require a month or more to cover, while other Units may be completed in a week or two. Many programs have found it to be very efficient to plot the curriculum on a calendar with "lesson days" interwoven with work days. Others have combined the Study Sills Curriculum lessons with other programs and curriculum such as social skills or vocational skills programs. Planning for a yearlong implementation schedule is critical to consistency and student success.

Contents

Notes:_____

Learning the ROPES Study Skills Curriculum: Scope and Sequence

Lessons and Activities	Materials

UNIT 1 Understanding Organizational Skills
Objectives
- Students will learn to use the Venn Diagram and other visual supports to organize personal information and get to know others.
- Students will discover that a Venn Diagram has multiple uses and is not just for use in Language Arts.
- Students will learn the skills that support good EF.
- The students will learn why EFS are important to success in school, home, and with their friends.
- Students will be introduced to various strategies to improve EFS.
- Students will self-evaluate their own organizational skills.

Lessons and Activities	Materials
Lesson 1: Using a Venn Diagram in a Novel Way **Activity 1:** Getting to Know Someone New, "An Icebreaker" **Optional Activity:** Unit 2, Lesson 1-Activity 4: Creating Student Binders	• Venn Diagram (ROPES-11) or; • Blank paper to draw Venn Diagram • White board and pens for demonstration • Student binder or folder to save all completed activity sheets • Timer to keep the lesson moving
Lesson 2: Identifying Executive Functioning Skills (EFS) **Activity 1:** Organizing Chaos Using EFS **Activity 2:** Identifying Reasons it is Important to be Organized **Activity 3:** Reasons Why it is Hard to Get Organized and Strategies that Help **Activity 4:** Explaining EFS **Activity 5:** Student Grading **Activity 6:** Establish a Class Reward System	• White board and markers or; • Chart paper and markers • T Chart forms (not on Download) or; • Blank paper to make a T Chart • Cluster Organizer (ROPES 01, 02, 03) • Executive Functioning Questionnaire (EFQ) (ROPES-Self-Evaluation) • Executive Functioning Questionnaire (EFQ) (ROPES-Teacher Evaluation) • Sample ROPES Goals • Summary of Strengths and Weaknesses Chart • Sequential Organizer (ROPES-04) • Task/Checklists (ROPES-05-05, 05-10, 05-15) • Venn Diagram (ROPES-11) • Basic Critical Thinking Skills Worksheet (ROPES-13). CST "Thinking Tool"
Lesson 3: Overview of the ROPES Components and the Executive Functioning Questionnaire (EFQ) **Activity 1:** Explaining ROPES Components **Activity 2:** Completing EFQ Self-Evaluation **Activity 3:** Identifying EF Strengths and Weaknesses **Activity 4:** Comparing Strengths and Weaknesses	• Executive Functioning Questionnaire (EFQ) (ROPES-Self-Evaluation) (Download) • Executive Functioning Questionnaire (EFQ) (ROPES-Teacher Evaluation) (Download) • Sample ROPES Goals (Download) • T CHART • Summary of Strengths and Weaknesses Chart • Venn Diagram (ROPES-11)
Lesson 4: Overview of Strategies: Graphic Organizers, Checklists, T Charts **Activity 1 :** Introduction to Graphic Organizers **Activity 2:** Making and Using Checklist **Optional Activity**: Daily Work Plan/Homework Plan Checklist	• Cluster Organizer (ROPES 01, 02, 03) • Sequential Organizer (ROPES-04) • Task/Checklists (ROPES-05-05, 05-10, 05-15) • Venn Diagram (ROPES-11) • Basic Critical Thinking Skills Worksheet (ROPES-13). CST "Thinking Tool" • T Chart

UNIT 2 Using External Supports: Organizing Space, Time, Work Tasks and Homework
Objectives
• Students will learn to use external supports including labels, containers, task boxes, timers, checklists, schedules, routines and other strategies to improve their organizational skills.
• Students will investigate the ways people organize their physical space and time and why it is important.
• Students will participate in binder and backpack organizational systems and routines that are followed regularly.
• Students will learn to use alarms and timers to structure *"opened ended"* tasks and to limit preferred activities.
• Students will learn to organize their work using Reminder Boards, Calendars, Schedules.

Lessons and Activities	Materials
Lesson 1: <u>Organizing Space</u> **Activity 1:** Identifying Organizational Supports **Activity 2:** Creating Organizational Supports **Activity 3:** Creating Student Supply Boxes **Activity 4:** Creating Student Binders **Activity 5:** Organizing Backpacks **Activity 6:** Sorting and Purging Backpacks	• Cluster Organizer (ROPES 01, 02, 03) • Task/Checklists (ROPES-05-05, 05-10, 05-15) • Venn Diagram (ROPES-11) • White Board And Markers • 2-3 inch binder for each student (or a 1-2 inch colored binder for each subject area) • Colored tabbed dividers with pockets for each student • Color coded homework folders for each student • 5 sheet protectors for each student • Colored book covers to coordinate with each colored tab divider or subject binder • Labels for binders and tab dividers
Lesson 2: <u>Organizing Time</u> **Activity 1:** Identifying Open verses Closed Activities **Activity 2:** Using Alarms and Timers in Open Ended Activities **Activity 3:** Using Alarms and Timers to Limit Preferred Activities	• Time Timer ® or other Visual Timer • Cell phone or tablets with Alarm reminder functions
Lesson 3: <u>Organizing Work</u> **Activity 1:** Using Reminder Boards and Notes to Self **Activity 2:** Using Monthly Calendars **Activity 3:** Using Checklists to Organize Tasks and Routines **Activity 4:** Using Daily Schedules	• Task/Checklists (ROPES-05-05, 05-10, 05-15) • Monthly Planning Calendar (ROPES-08) • Daily Schedule (ROPES-09) • Post-it Notes • Mini Notebook • Reminder Board
Lesson 4: <u>Using Homework Management Systems</u> **Activity 1:** Using Homework Folders **Activity 2:** Using and Checking the Student Planner/Log	• Work Plan Form • Colored Folders with two pockets • Labels • Homework Summary Page (ROPES 06) • Homework Summary Page (ROPES 07) or: • School adopted planner

Lessons and Activities	Materials
UNIT 3: Evaluating Actions and Outcomes **Objectives** • Students will learn strategies to evaluate actions and choices in order to make good decisions with positive outcomes. • Students will learn to predict outcomes in novel and familiar situations and then choose appropriate actions that result in positive or desirable outcomes. • Students will also learn a process to reflect on behaviors that interfere with school or social success.	
Lesson 1: Reflecting on Past Actions and Choices **Activity 1:** Evaluating Good Choices, "Daily Pat on the Back"	• Basic Critical Thinking Skills Worksheet (ROPES-13). CST "Thinking Tool"
Lesson 2: Choice Making **Activity 1:** Making Good Choices	• Basic Critical Thinking Skills Worksheet (ROPES-13). CST "Thinking Tool" • Goals Worksheet (ROPES-14) • Evaluating and Selecting Appropriate Actions (ROPES-20).
Lesson 3: Goal Setting **Activity 1:** Setting Personal Goals **Activity 2:** Identifying Areas for Self-Improvement	• Basic Critical Thinking Skills Worksheet (ROPES-13). CST "Thinking Tool" • Goals Worksheet (ROPES-14) • Evaluating and Selecting Appropriate Actions (ROPES-20). • Action Plan Cards (ROPES 21)
Lesson 4: Problem Solving **Activity 1:** Reflecting on Individual Student Behavior	• Basic Critical Thinking Skills Worksheet (ROPES-13). CST "Thinking Tool" • Goals Worksheet (ROPES-14) • Evaluating and Selecting Appropriate Actions (ROPES-20). • Action Plan Cards (ROPES 21) • Evaluating and Resolving Problem Behavior (ROPES 17) • Behavior Problem Solving Worksheet (ROPES 18-19) • Self Improvement Contract (ROPES 24)

Lessons and Activities	Materials
UNIT 4: Organizing Information from Lecture and Written Materials **Objectives** • Students will learn how to use graphic organizers to help them better recall and organize information so it can be integrated with other knowledge for functional use. • They will learn to summarize information based on their experiences, what they hear and what they read.	
Lessons and Activities	**Materials**
<u>**Lesson 1** : Using Graphic Organizers to Summarize and Recall Personal Experiences and Events</u> **Activity 1:** Definition of a Summary ***The following activities will use T Charts to:*** **Activity 2:** Summarize Tasks and Instructions **Activity 3:** Recall Previous Experiences **Activity 4:** Write a Summary about a Personal Experience **Activity 5:** Summarize a Personal Experience **Activity 6:** Give an Oral Summary of a Personal Experience **Activity 7:** Write a Summary about a Personal Experience	• T Charts
<u>**Lesson 2:** Creating Written Summaries from Lectures and Taking Notes</u> ***The following activities will use T Charts to:*** **Activity 1:** Summarize Information from Lectures **Activity 2:** Create Oral Summaries from Lectures **Activity 3:** Create Written Summaries from Lectures **Activity 4:** Summarize Information from Written Text **Activity 5:** Create Oral Summaries from Text **Activity 6:** Write Summaries from Text	• 6-8 selected paragraphs on various topics, preferably from student textbooks or current events • White boards • T Charts • Photo copies of text passages

UNIT 5: Time Management and Prioritization **Objectives** • Students will learn to estimate the amount of time activities will take to complete. • Students will learn to prioritize activities. • Students will learn to set short and long term goals.	
Lessons and Activities	**Materials**
<u>Lesson 1:</u> Time Estimations and "Guesstimations" **Activity 1:** Time Estimations **Activity 2:** "Guesstimations" **Activity 3:** Determining "Work Time" for Homework	• Time Journal (ROPES-10). • Venn Diagram (ROPES-11). • Basic Critical Thinking Skills Worksheet (Ropes-13). CST "Thinking Tool" • Goals Worksheet (ROPES-14). • Decision Matrix for Prioritization (ROPES -13). • Priorities Ladder (ROPES -13). • Monthly Planning Calendars (ROPES -18), • Daily Schedules (ROPES -09). • Timers • T Chart
<u>Lesson 2:</u> Prioritization of Activities and Tasks **Activity 1:** Determining Priorities **Activity 2:** Using the Decision Matrix for Prioritization **Activity 3:** Using a Priorities Ladder for Decision Making	• Decision Matrix for Prioritization (ROPES-13). • Basic Critical Thinking Skills Worksheet (ROPES-13). CST "Thinking Tool" • Priorities Ladder (ROPES-16)
<u>Lesson 3:</u> Using a Calendar to Plot Goals **Activity 1:** Creating Monthly Planning Calendars **Activity 2:** Creating a Daily Schedule Based on Monthly Planning Calendar **Activity 3:** Using a Calendar to Plot Short and Long Term Goals	• Goals Worksheet (ROPES-14). • Decision Matrix for Prioritization (ROPES-13). • Priorities Ladder (ROPES-16) • Monthly Planning Calendars (ROPES -18), • Homework Summary Page (ROPES 06-07)

UNIT 6: Project Management **Objectives** • Students will learn to organize a long term project using organizational tools including graphic organizers, binders, folders, checklists, and calendars. • Students will learn to organize an individual project using organizational tools including graphic organizers, binders, folders, checklists, and calendars.	
Lessons and Activities	**Materials**
Lesson 1: Planning and Implementing a Group Project **Activity 1:** Brainstorming Project Ideas **Activity 2:** Evaluate Project Ideas **Activity 3:** Chunking the Project **Activity 4:** Prioritizing Chunks **Activity 5:** Creating Action Plans and To-do Lists **Activity 6:** Execute the Plan and Self-Monitor Progress	• Basic Critical Thinking Skills Worksheet (ROPES-13). CST "Thinking Tool" • T Charts • Cluster Organizers (ROPES-01, 02, 03). • Organization And Planning Worksheets (ROPES-12) • Action Planning Cards (ROPES-21) • To Do Lists • Checklist (ROPES 05-05, 05-10, 05-15) • Monthly Planning Calendar (ROPES-08) • Project Binder Or Folder With Tabs • Self Evaluation Rubric
Lesson 2: Planning and Implementing an Individual Project **Activities 1-6** listed for Lesson 1 repeated	• Repeat use of forms above

UNIT 7: Self-Awareness, Self-Monitoring and Self-Management
Objectives

- Students will become aware of their strengths and weaknesses and learn to advocate for assistance when needed.
- Students will learn to use supports to improve their ability to self-evaluate, monitor and manage their reactions and behaviors in a variety of situations.
- Students will learn to use external visual supports and graphic organizers to improve their ability to self-manage stress and frustration in a variety of situations.
- Students will learn to request needed assistance and resources across various situations to assist them in coping with challenges and obstacles.

Lessons and Activities	Materials
Lesson 1: Increasing Self Awareness **Activity 1:** Determining Sharing, and Summarizing Strengths and Weaknesses **Activity 2:** Self-Monitoring On and Off Task Behaviors **Activity 3:** Increasing On Task Time in Class	• Self Evaluation Stress Triggers (ROPES 25) • Self Evaluation Efficiency (ROPES 26) • EFQ Self Evaluation • Timer • T Charts
Lesson 2: Self-Managing Undesired or Problematic Behaviors **Activity 1:** Selecting a Behavior to Change and Collecting Baseline **Activity 2:** Using Self-Improvement Contracts to Change a Target Behavior	• Completed EFQ Self Evaluation • Previous Quarter's Grades • T Chart • Self-Improvement Contract (ROPES 24)
Lesson 3: Self-Management of Stress and Frustration **Activity 1:** Managing Stress and Frustration	• Basic Critical Thinking Skills Worksheet (ROPES-13). CST "Thinking Tool" • Self Evaluation Stress Triggers (ROPES 25)
Lesson 4: Self-Management of Efficiency **Activity 1:** Improving Efficiency	• Time Journal (ROPES-10 • Self Evaluation Efficiency (ROPES 26) • Self-Improvement Contract (ROPES 24)
Lesson 5: Self-Advocacy **Activity 1:** Improving Self-Advocacy	• A variety of real life situations • T Chart

Notes:

Unit 1: Understanding Organizational Skills

Objectives

- Students will learn to use the VENN DIAGRAM and other visual supports to organize personal information and get to know others.
- Students will discover that a VENN DIAGRAM has multiple uses and is not just for use in Language Arts.
- Students will learn the skills that support good EF.
- The students will learn why EFS are important to success in school, home, and with their friends.
- Students will be introduced to various strategies to improve EFS.
- Students will self-evaluate their own organizational skills.

Content for Teachers

It is important for students to feel like an active participant in the content and process of the "Study Skills Curriculum". The students need to be a part of establishing the rules, expectations, grading and outcomes for the study skills class. The following lessons are designed to develop a personal understanding of EF within the class group and in various formats. The activities will provide concrete visual formats to assist in establishing the rules, expectations and grading/outcomes for the study skills class. The lessons and activities in this unit should be done during the first week of class. These lessons are ongoing and designed to be embedded in all educational settings.

Lesson 1: Using a VENN DIAGRAM in a Novel Way

Unit 1: Lesson 1

Materials

- Printed copies of VENN DIAGRAM (ROPES-11) for every student or;
- Blank paper for students to draw their own VENN DIAGRAM
- White board and pens for demonstration
- Student binder or folder to save all completed activity sheets
- Timer to keep the lesson moving

Lesson 1-Activity 1: *Getting to Know Someone New, "An Icebreaker"*

Set Up

Hand out VENN DIAGRAMS to students. Select a student volunteer to model the process. Have a timer ready to set for 3-5 minutes after the explanation and demonstration of the activity. This activity may take place during the first 10-15 minutes of the class period for the first few days of the semester.

Steps for Demonstration

1. Ask for a student to volunteer so this activity can be modeled for the whole class.
2. On the whiteboard, draw a VENN DIAGRAM similar to the student handout.
3. Write the teacher's name on one side of the diagram and the student's name on the other side.
4. The teacher asks a series of questions to the volunteer and writes the answers on the VENN DIAGRAM.
   a. Questions such as "What do you like to do for fun, relaxation, entertainment?", "What is your favorite movie, restaurant, food, song, band, dessert, place to vacation" etc.
   b. These types of questions can be written on the board as prompts.
5. Record the responses that are unique to the teacher on one side.
6. Record the student's unique responses on the other side of the diagram.
7. Common answers, should be recorded in the middle of the VENN DIAGRAM.
   a. Point out that the items in center are what two people have in common.
   b. Mention that these shared interests/topics may become a basis for conversations and friendships.

Figure 1.1

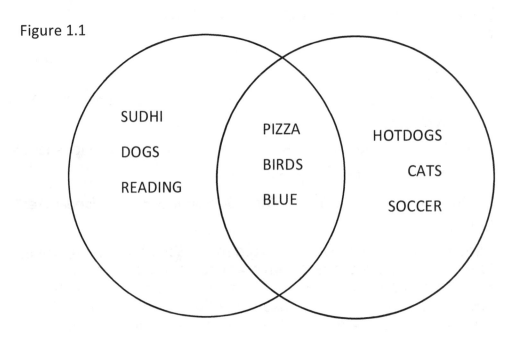

Steps for Participation

8. Instruct the students to find a partner and ask questions to get to know the other person.

9. Remind the students to follow the steps in the demonstration.

   a. Write their names and the names of their partners on the VENN DIAGRAM.

   b. Write the corresponding answers that are unique to themselves and their partner under their names and common items in the center.

10. Set a timer for five minutes

    a. Time extension may be required for the first activity to allow enough time for the students to gathered at least three areas of common interest in the center of the VENN DIAGRAM.

11. When the time is up, the students should take turns introducing their partners to the class sharing one thing that is unique about that person, the items in the outer circle, and one item in the *center*, a common interest. Some students may need written scripted questions to guide the activity.

Debrief Activity

1. Ask the students why they think they used the VENN DIAGRAM for this activity as opposed to having a conversation with the other person.

2. Ask students to share how the VENN DIAGRAM helped them.

   a. Explain that the visual supports, such as this graphic organizer, help to "Structure" and "Organize" information. These concepts will be introduced more formally in later lessons, but can be discussed if time allows.

3. Repeat process with every student and staff in class until each team has gathered three pieces of information they have in common with each other (center of the VENN DIAGRAM).

4. This may be completed in one class time or over several days depending on the variables in the class

5. Students should keep these diagrams in a binder or folder for later reference.

| Unit 1: Lesson 2 | **Lesson 2: Identifying Executive Functioning Skills (EFS)** |

Materials

- White board and markers or;
- Chart paper and markers
- T CHART forms or;
- Blank paper to make a T CHART

Lesson 2-Activity 1: *Organizing Chaos Using Executive Functioning Skills*

Set Up

Prior to students entering the classroom, rearrange the room to create chaos and disorganization. For example, turn over desks, put papers and trash on the floor, put books on chairs, turn over chairs, put chairs on desks, etc.

Steps for Participation

1. As the students enter the classroom, tell them you will return in five minutes and you expect them to, "Be ready for class." Do not give any further explanation of what "Be ready" means.

2. After five minutes return to the classroom to see what has been done. If nothing has changed or if the room is still in a state of chaos, restate that you will be back in five minutes and expect them to "Be ready," and be more direct this time!

3. If the room is put back together and students have arranged the environment to "Be ready to learn" give them some specific praise about their ability to make order out of chaos.

Debrief Activity

1. Ask students how they felt when they arrived at class today.
   a. List their feelings on a T CHART on the left hand side.
   b. List all feelings the students identify, which should include responses like confused, anxious, nervous, etc.

2. Ask students to describe what made them have these feelings.
   a. Write their responses on the right side of the T CHART.
   b. Try to elicit words such as chaos, disorder, disorganized, unexpected, confused, etc.

3. Ask "What did you do to solve the problem?"
   a. Make another T CHART and write down the responses to this question on the left side.

b. Try to elicit responses such as, planned what to do, organized the space, took on certain roles in the group, worked together, add-asked questions, asked for a plan, asked for help,etc.

4. Ask students to describe how they feel now that the classroom is organized. Write their responses on the other side of the T CHART.

5. Point out how chaos and disorganization relate to many negative feelings and that order and organization relate to more positive feelings.

   a. Explain that we all do our best when we are in a positive state of mind and that being in an orderly and organized situation helps us all.

6. Explain that the way they identified and solved the problem of making order out of chaos is called Executive Functioning Skills (EFS). Write ROPES on the board and tell students what each letter represents. Show them how they used the ROPES to solve the current problem.

7. You had to Recall what an organized classroom looks like

8. You had to Organize the environment and the people

9. You had to Plan who would do what and Prioritize what to do first, second, third...

10. You had to Evaluate what was most important

11. And you had to Self-Manage and monitor what was happening as there was no adult there to guide you

12. Explain how this class is all about teaching students how to make a plan and get organized to avoid and overcome feelings of frustration and anxiety. The class is about learning the ROPES to Improve Executive Functioning Skills (EFS)!

Lesson 2-Activity 2: Identifying Reasons it is Important to be Organized

Set Up

Group the students in pairs. Have chart paper and pens ready to record the students *Reasons it is Important to be Organized*.

Steps for Participation

1. Ask the students to share with a partner several reasons why it is important to be organized and have plans.

   a. Be sure to prompt and guide certain ideas such as: to be a successful student, to turn in assignments on time, to keep track of important items, to set goals and reach them, to pass classes, to get a job in the future, adult recognition and praise, etc.

2. Record the reasons on chart paper.
3. Post the chart of reasons they have developed for access and later class use.
4. Refer and add to this chart regularly, reminding the students of the reasons why they determined that organization is so critical.

Lesson 2-Activity 3: *Why Organization and Planning are Hard and Identifying Strategies to Help*
Set Up
Review T CHART list of reasons why the students determined that organization is important.

Materials
- White board and markers
- CLUSTER ORGANIZER forms (ROPES 01, 02, 03)

Steps for Participation
1. Pass out two blank CLUSTER ORGANIZERS to each student.
2. Draw a CLUSTER ORGANIZER on the board with a center circle and several supporting circles.
   a. In the center cluster write "reasons organization may be hard."
3. Since the students know why it is so important to be organized, ask them why it is often such a challenge?
4. Record students' responses in the supporting circles on the board. Sample responses for the outer circles could be:
   a. Some people have disabilities or learning differences,
   b. There are too many distractions,
   c. Students were never taught strategies to get organized,
   d. No money or resources to buy a calendar or timer,
   e. Too much information or stuff to retain,
   f. Not enough time to get organized etc.
   g. It's too hard, too much to remember,
   h. Don't know where to start.

Figure 1.2 Cluster Organizer Sample "Why is Organization Hard?"

5. Have the students copy down answers from the board onto their own CLUSTER ORGANIZER in the supporting circles.

6. Draw a second CLUSTER ORGANIZER on the board and repeat the same process but instead in the center circle write "strategies that help" to get and stay organized.

7. In the supporting circles write student responses and include examples such as:

   a. Write things down, use color coding, use labels, use a timer, use folders, learn to ask for help, use calendars and planners, dividers, hooks, hangers, containers, signs, bins, be willing to learn, have a teacher help check up on you, CHECKLISTS, etc.

Figure 1.3 Cluster Organizers Sample "Strategies that HELP"

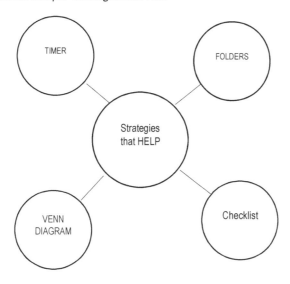

8. Discuss strategies and barriers. Acknowledge the barriers and obstacles but also offer solutions and rationales for how and why these barriers can be overcome.

9. Explain to students that this class is designed to help them learn *effective strategies* to use when faced with difficult or confusing situations.

   a. Be sure to write solutions on the board and have students keep a list they can access and add to throughout the semester.

10. Have the students file the CLUSTER ORGANIZERS in their binders or folders for later reference.

Lesson 2-Activity 4: *Explaining Executive Functioning (EF)*

Set Up

If possible have a video clip of an orchestra tuning up and a clip of an orchestra playing in harmony.

Materials

• White board and markers

Steps for Participation

1. Explain that the thinking skills and behaviors involved in being organized are called Executive Functioning (EF).

2. Introduce the idea of the band/orchestra conductor. Describe how all of the instruments are there, and how the conductor helps them organize their timing so that it is pleasant sounding.

   a. Ask students if the have you ever heard a band warming up prior to an event?

   b. Have students describe this and ask, "Why do you think it sounds so awful?"

   c. Play audio of an orchestra tuning up and then playing in harmony.

   d. Point out that the difference is that someone (the conductor) is organizing the band.

3. Explain that EF is like the orchestra conductor.

   a. Ask students what they think the role of a band conductor is. List examples on the board. Explain that if the orchestra conductor did not exist, the orchestra could NOT get organized or work in unison. This is what happens when EF skills are not used or are underdeveloped.

   b. Explain that EF helps a student to initiate tasks, self-monitor, control emotions and impulses, use memory effectively (recall), be flexible, shift between activities, plan, organize, set goals, deal with novel situations and organize time.

c. Explain that certain learning differences make EF skills more challenging to learn, including ADD/ADHD, Autism Spectrum Disorders and some learning disabilities.

d. If students have underdeveloped EF skills, they may struggle to be organized, complete work, and be successful in school.

4. Provide examples that illustrate "Executive Controls" like an air traffic controller, an administrative assistant to a CEO, a Principal, etc. You may give other examples that illustrate the need for someone to organize in order for things to run smoothly.

Lesson 2-Activity 5: Student Grading

Set Up

Prepare a rubric format of the core skills that are being taught in this class. This rubric will be used to establish an individual grading/point system to determine student grades. This should be done as a whole class activity during the first week of class.

Steps for Participation

1. When developing the definitions of core areas, use a T CHART to provide examples and non-examples of each skill area.

a. Ask the whole class to define each core area with a point value assigned to different levels of performance. For example, the definition of punctual means to be on time, sitting quietly in chair at bell with materials out and ready to participate. Punctual does NOT mean, standing at bell, not having materials out, talking, etc.

b. It is most meaningful if the students identify the examples, non-examples and definitions for the rubric.

2. This rubric should be used on a daily basis to assign points to each student for their class grade.

a. Initially, within the first two weeks of class, the teacher will assign the points to each student at the end of each class period with an explanation of how/why the assigned point value was earned.

3. After the initial two weeks, the students should begin to self-evaluate.

a. At the end of each class period, the teacher should ask the students what they earned and why. If there is an agreement, bonus points can be assigned or class reward points can be earned (see below).

4. If a student is consistently scoring 0 – 1 in a core area, the teacher should schedule a student conference to discuss issues and develop an individual student support plan.

Figure 1.4: Sample Rubric

Core Skill	0	1	2	Total
Punctual	Late to class.	On time to class, but not sitting in desk, no planner or required materials out at bell or talking when bell rang.	On time, sitting quietly in chair at bell with materials out and ready to participate.	
Organized	Did not have items needed for class, personal space (backpack/binder/desk) were disorganized or messy.	Had materials but could not locate or find all needed items. Personal space (backpack/binder/desk) was partially in order.	Had and could easily locate items. Personal space was highly organized and neat.	
Participation	Did not participate in group activities. Did not use time in class effectively to complete personal work plan. Did not use supports or strategies taught in class (planner, work plans, etc.)	Partially participated in group activities. Used some class time effectively to complete personal work plan. Used some of the strategies taught in class (planner, work plans, etc.)	Made effective use of all class time including completing personal work plan and fully participating in group activities. Consistently used all of the strategies taught in class (planner, schedule, work plan, timers, organizational routines, etc.)	

Lesson 2-Activity 6: *Establish a Class Reward System*
Set Up

In order to promote teamwork, positive interactions and peer to peer encouragement, a whole class reward system should be established. Draw a CLUSTER ORGANIZER on the board. In the center circle write "Class Reward System".

Steps for Participation

1. Ask students to brainstorm ideas of what might be earned by the class for making progress and working well as a team.
   a. These should be items or activities that can be earned over a period of 4-6 weeks of class time (e.g. at the end of each grading period).
   b. Examples include: pizza party, game day, movie day, etc.
   c. Record ideas on the board using a CLUSTER ORGANIZER.

2. Ask students to select their most preferred of the choices by putting a tally mark next to their choice activity.
   a. After each student votes, identify the item the group will work toward for the next 4-6 weeks or until the preset number of points are accumulated.

3. With teacher guidance, have the students generate a list of 4-6 expectations for earning Class Reward Points. Examples could include:

  a. *Be honest with yourself and others:* This includes accurately identify your strengths and needs, grading yourself fairly and accurately, etc.

  b. *Be a supportive peer:* Help other students with activities, assignments or participation.

  c. *Be a good group member:* Wait for your turn, use kind words, participate and share ideas with the group, stay on topic. The teacher should adjust the wording and complexity to the needs and abilities of the students.

Lesson 3: Overview of the ROPES Components and the Executive Functioning Questionnaire (EFQ) | **Unit 1: Lesson 3**

Materials

- EXECUTIVE FUNCTIONING QUESTIONNAIRE (EFQ) (ROPES-SELF-EVALUATION) for each student
- EXECUTIVE FUNCTIONING QUESTIONNAIRE (EFQ) (ROPES-TEACHER EVALUATION)
- Sample ROPES GOALS
- T CHART
- Summary of Strengths and Weaknesses Chart

Lesson 3-Activity 1: *Explain the R.O.P.E.S. Components*
Set Up

Use a white board or chart paper to complete this activity with the whole class.

Steps for Participation

1. Explain to the students that the purpose of the class is to teach organizational strategies that will provide them with the necessary structure and support to overcome challenges associated with EFS.

2. Review the Components of "The ROPES" that were introduced in Lesson 2, Activity 1. The core executive functioning skills are:

  a. **R**ecalling and restating information in meaningful ways.

  b. **O**rganization and planning skills.

  c. **P**lanning, **P**rioritizing and goal directed behavior.

  d. **E**valuating situations, actions and outcomes.

  e. **S**elf-management.

3. Write out each letter on board and underneath each letter write down and/or brainstorm how these skills are used at school.

   a. **Recall:** Remembering past experiences, information for tests and comprehension questions, due dates, home-work, etc.

   b. **Organization:** Finding materials, organizing ideas for papers and projects, sorting and cleaning up (backpack, locker, etc.)

   c. **Planning and Prioritizing:** Knowing the steps for task completion and getting tasks done on time, making choices to work before play, (what you have to do be-fore what you want to do)

   d. **Evaluating:** Making good choices, setting goals, prob-lem solving, determining if something worked well or did not work at all

   e. **Self-Management:** Being independent and able to man age a situation without help or an adult monitoring you

4. Explain to students that they will be expected to become independent in managing their time, activities and school-work. It is important that the students understand that the goal of this class is to give them strategies that can help them be successful in school, at home, with their friends, and eventually in college and/or careers.

5. Draw a T CHART on the board. Ask students to identify things that they get in trouble for with teachers, peers and parents. Write issues on left side of T CHART.

   a. Examples: missing assignments, incomplete work, los-ing work/things, being messy, not trying, being critical of others, not thinking before talking, etc.

6. Evaluate each troublesome issue and ask students to iden-tify which part of the ROPES would help.

   a. Record the component from the ROPES that would be helpful in the right column of the T CHART.

   b. Title each column as follows: Left side of T CHART *"Problems"* and the Right side of T CHART *"Skills and Strategies to Learn"*.

   c. After there are several items in each column ask the students to make a personal choice between "Getting in trouble for the challenges listed in the left column OR learning new skills and strategies to help them be more successful".

Lesson 3-Activity 2: *Completing the EXECUTIVE FUNCTIONING QUESTIONNAIRE (EFQ)*
Set Up

Print an EXECUTIVE FUNCTIONING QUESTIONNAIRE (EFQ) (ROPES-Self-Evaluation) for each student.

Materials

- EXECUTIVE FUNCTIONING QUESTIONNAIRE (EFQ) (ROPES-Self-Evaluation)
- EXECUTIVE FUNCTIONING QUESTIONNAIRE (EFQ) (ROPES-Teacher Evaluation) this is used for the Parent as well.

Steps for Participation

1. Each student should complete the EFQ Self-Evaluation of their own EF Skills (EFS) within a group activity format.

2. Read each item to the whole class and give examples to ensure each student understands characteristics to be evaluated.

3. Explain the rating scale. Giving multiple examples to ensure understanding.

4. Have students score themselves on each item.

5. Give each student 2-3 copies of the EFQ for their teachers and parents to use to provide input as well.

   a. Assign students to have their parents and 2-3 of their teachers complete the EFQ Teacher-Evaluation form on them. Teachers can be current teachers or past teachers who know the student well.

   b. These are to be collected by the student and returned to class within one week.

6. Additional Assessment Options: For purposes of objective evaluation and progress monitoring, school staff may also want to administer a standardized assessment of EFS such as the *Behavior Rating Inventory of Executive Function® (BRIEF®)* or components of *A Developmental NEuroPSYchological Assessment (NEPSY)*.

Lesson 3-Activity 3: *Identifying EF Strengths and Weaknesses*
Set Up

The students will need their completed EXECUTIVE FUNCTIONING QUESTIONNAIRE (EFQ) (ROPES-Self Evaluation). Provide students with a T CHART form or blank paper to draw their own T CHART.

Materials

- T CHART form or blank paper

Steps for Participation

1. Using their own completed EFQ Self-Evaluation ask the students to complete a T CHART identifying their strengths and weaknesses.
   a. Strengths would be items with a score of 2 or 3 (list on the left side of T CHART).
   b. Weaknesses would be items with scores of 0 or 1 (list on the right side of T CHART).
2. Ask students to identify 1-2 areas they would like to work on improving in the coming weeks.
   a. Have students write a sentence about what they want to improve and why on the bottom of the T CHART form.
   b. Ask students to share their goal area with the class or a partner.
3. Have students keep the T CHART in their binders.
4. The teacher should keep the original questionnaires and have students and their teachers/parents complete a second EFQ at the end of the school year, or semester if this is a semester long class. This is a good method for evaluating growth over time.

Lesson 3-Activity 4: *Comparing Strengths and Weaknesses*
Set Up

Students will need their completed T CHART from Lesson 3-Activity 3 that outlines their relative strengths and weaknesses in EF and a VENN DIAGRAM form or blank paper to draw a VENN DIAGRAM

Materials

- VENN DIAGRAM form or blank paper

Steps for Participation

1. Reflect on the idea that everyone has strengths and weaknesses. Using a T CHART on the board, the teacher should identify personal strengths and weaknesses and share these with students.
2. Introduce the idea that it is good to know that others have strengths and weaknesses that are different from our own.
   a. Explain that when people know each other's strengths and weaknesses they can work together to support one another.

    b. Have students work with a partner and compare their lists of strengths and weaknesses.

3. Have students share their strengths and weakness with a partner using a VENN DIAGRAM.

    a. Have students write their individual strengths (scores of 2 or 3) in the outer edges of the VENN DIAGRAM.

    b. Have students write their "shared" strengths in the center of the VENN DIAGRAM.

4. Point out that it is important to know when others have strengths that we may not have.

    a. We can all learn from others.

    b. In this class it is encouraged that everyone learns from each another.

5. Repeat procedure with weaknesses.

6. Have them discuss ways that they could support one another based on each person's strengths and weaknesses.

    a. Methods of support may be recorded on a chart for future reference.

Lesson 4: Overview of Strategies: Graphic Organizers, Checklists, T Charts　　　**Unit 1: Lesson 4**

Content Information for Teachers

The graphic organizer is "a visual representation of knowledge" (Bromley, K., Irwin-DeVitas, L., and Modlo, M., 1995). Graphic organizers facilitate learning by helping students organize ideas and see relationships between different pieces of information. Research has shown that "creating and using graphic organizers to illustrate the organization of ideas and information aids comprehension and learning" (Flood, J., and Lapp, D., 1988; Heimlich, J., and Pittelman, S., 1986).

Graphic organizers have been shown to be effective with a wide variety of learners, including those with learning disabilities and Autism Spectrum Disorders (ASD). The aim is to "provide the learner with a system that is easy to use but that they will find useful and valuable in many ways for the rest of their lives" (Pehrsson, R., and Denner, P., 1989).

Although the typical use of graphic organizers is to address specific academic tasks, this Study Skill Curriculum will be utilizing graphic organizers in a very different way. The graphic organizers will be used as a strategy students will develop to support improved organizational skills and organized thinking.

Materials
- CLUSTER ORGANIZER (ROPES-01, 02, 03)
- SEQUENTIAL ORGANIZER (ROPES-04)
- TASK/CHECKLISTS (ROPES-05-05, 05-10, 05-15)
- VENN DIAGRAM (ROPES-11)
- BASIC CRITICAL THINKING SKILLS WORKSHEET (ROPES-13). Circle-Square-Triangle (CST) "Thinking Tool"
- T CHART

Lesson 4-Activity 1: *Introduction to Graphic Organizers*
Set Up

Write the five types of graphic organizers on the board (VENN DIAGRAM DIAGRAMS, TASK/CHECKLISTS, T CHARTS, CLUSTER ORGANIZERS, and the BASIC CRITICAL THINKING SKILLS WORK-SHEET (CST "Thinking Tool")

Steps for Participation
1. Give a brief example of each type and have students discuss when they have used them or seen them used.
2. Be prepared to give multiple choice answers if they can't generate their own.
3. CLUSTER ORGANIZERS: This type of organizer states knowledge and shows how different parts pertain to the whole.
   a. It is good to use when integrating new knowledge with previously learned material and when "brainstorming" a topic or idea.
   b. It is also useful when attempting to break down specific skills or topics into component parts.
   c. Using this type of graphic organizer is often called "webbing."

Figure 1.5 Cluster Organizer Sample

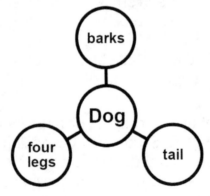

4. SEQUENTIAL ORGANIZERS: These organizers depict action sequences.

   a. They demonstrate the order or progression of a partic-ular act or situation.

   b. They are very useful for prioritizing or putting parts in a logical order for a particular desired outcome.

   c. Figure 1.6 is an example of a SEQUENTIAL ORGANIZER:

Figure 1.6 Basic Critical Thinking Skills Worksheet (ROPES-13). CST "Thinking Tool"

5. VENN DIAGRAM: This type of organizer is often used to show relationships between ideas.

   a. It is useful for examining similarities and differences and it is frequently used as a pre-writing activity to enable students to organize thoughts prior to writing a compare/contrast essay.

Figure 1.7 Example of a VENN DIAGRAM (ROPES-11)

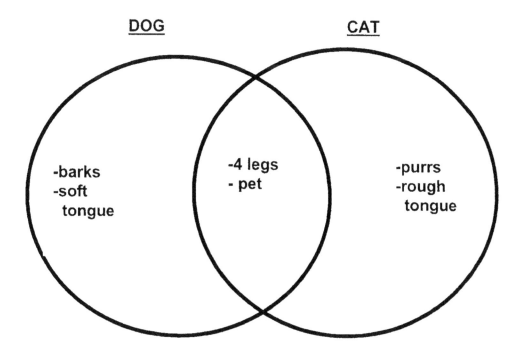

6. CHECKLISTS: This is a type of SEQUENTIAL ORGANIZER that allows the user to indicate the completion of various steps within a larger task.

Figure 1.8 SEQUENTIAL ORGANIZER checklist

Routine Checklist

Nighttime Routine Checklist

Done

Shower ☐

Get Dressed (night clothes) ☐

Brush teeth ☐

Set alarm clock ☐

Go to bed ☐

Reviewed By: ☐

7. T CHARTS: A T CHART is used to organize information about two topics or main ideas. This differs from a VENN DIAGRAM because the two topics are unrelated.

T CHART Mac vs PC

Mac	PC
Fewer viruses	Less expensive
Fast processor	More people have them
Coordinates with other APPLE products	More software programs available
	Windows OS

Figure 1.9 Sample T Chart

Lesson 4-Activity 2: *Making and Using CHECKLISTS*

Materials

- CHECKLISTS and WORK PLANNING FORM

Content Information for Teachers

CHECKLISTS are strategies for teaching students to compensate for problems with shifting attention and working memory. Students are first taught how to use the check list: crossing off or checking off the steps as they are completed. Once they are successful at using the CHECKLISTS, they should be taught how to independently create them.

Set Up

Be prepared to share CHECKLISTS you use.

Steps for Participation

1. Explain to students what CHECKLISTS are and that everyone uses lists to aid with remembering things and staying organized.

2. Ask students to brainstorm different things where a CHECKLIST could be helpful to them in their everyday lives, such as shopping lists, to do lists, packing for a trip, chores, etc.

3. Draw a CLUSTER ORGANIZER on the board and write the name of a specific task in the center.

   a. Choose a simple and concrete task like making a peanut butter and jelly (PB&J) sandwich.

4. Brainstorm components of this task and write them in the outer circles.

   a. Do not worry about the order in which students tell you the components of the task, simply write what students say.

5. After the task components are brainstormed, show students how to convert the information into a sequential CHECKLIST.

   a. If time allows, have students use their CHECKLIST to make a PB&J sandwich following the CHECKLIST exactly as they developed it to see how it turned out.

   b. If there are steps that are missing, such as cleaning up or getting certain items, have the students add the steps to the CHECKLIST.

6. Show multiple samples of CHECKLISTS to the students.
   a. Ask them to evaluate the CHECKLISTS to see if there are any steps missing.
7. Once the students have the process down for using CHECKLISTS, work with them to initiate the use of CHECKLISTS independently. Bonus points may be a good motivator.
8. Next, have students choose a partner and develop an end of school day CHECKLIST.
   a. This may be done individually based on the individual student's needs.
9. Have students share their CHECKLISTS with the group.
10. HOMEWORK: Have students use their end of day CHECK-LIST that day and come prepared to discuss the experience the following day. Award class points for completing and using the end of day CHECKLIST.

Ready To Go Home Routine Check List	Done
Take out Homework Summary Page	☐
Get all needed materials	☐
Put materials in backpack	☐
Put Homework Summary Page in backpack	☐
Collect any items in "Out Box"	☐
Put them in backpack	☐
Chose a free time activity to do while waiting for the bus	☐
Reviewed By: ☐	

Figure 1.10 Sample Checklist

Optional Activity: *Study Skills Class - Daily Work Plan CHECKLIST*

If the students have class time for work completion during Study Skills Class, have them develop an In Class Work To Do Plan and a Homework Work Plan CHECKLIST. Assign students to this as they complete work that day or that night for homework.

Steps for Participation

1. Inform students that work completion is often a task that requires a CHECKLIST in order to stay organized.

2. Show students how to develop a DAILY WORK PLAN by writing down what work needs to be done that day/night for homework to be turned in the following day. Information from the students' planner should be referenced in addition to daily homework assignments.

3. Each day, as part of the Study Skills Class, have students complete a DAILY WORK PLAN. This can be work that they will do in class if you have time for curriculum support, or items that they will complete for homework that night.

4. Work through the process with the students observing and answering specific questions about why certain tasks need to get done and discuss their logical order.

   a. Students will eventually take over the process of filling out the DAILY WORK PLAN based on the time estimated for each activity and the priorities for the day which will be discussed in later units.

5. Award class points for developing the work plan on the day it is developed.

   a. Award points for using and completing their work on the DAILY WORK PLAN once the work is completed (e.g. at the end of the class period if you run curriculum support or the next day if the DAILY WORK PLAN was for nightly homework).

Figure 1.11

STUDY SKILLS CLASS - DAILY WORK PLAN

NAME: _____ DATE: _____

IN CLASS WORK TO DO:	FINISHED

HOMEWORK WORK PLAN	FINISHED

COMMENTS:

Unit 2: Using External Supports:
Organizing Space, Time, Work Tasks and Homework

Objective

- Students will learn to use external supports including labels, containers, task boxes, timers, CHECKLISTS, schedules, routines and other strategies to improve their organizational skills.

- Students will investigate the ways people organize their physical space and time and the reasons why organization is important.

- Students will participate in binder and backpack organizational systems and routines that are followed regularly.

- Students will learn to use alarms and timers to structure *"open-ended"* tasks and to limit preferred activities.

- Students will learn to organize work using Reminder Boards, Calendars, Schedules.

Content Information for Teachers

Think about how you organize your kitchen, garage, closet, office or other important areas in your home. How we arrange and organize our space can either help us to access information we need easily and without frustration, or it can result in us spending unnecessary time searching, hunting and feeling frustrated because we cannot find the items we need. Using external supports in the classroom and teaching students how to use good physical and visual structure are essential for students to reach their highest potential.

The physical layout of an area can either promote attention, organization and efficiency or detract from it. By carefully arranging the learning environment and providing external organizational supports, we can prevent many of the behavioral challenges and learning issues related to Executive Dysfunction. Keep in mind that developmentally, students learn how to organize their external environment prior to learning how to organize their internal world such as their thoughts, activities and feelings. Children are taught to categorize items while cleaning up their toys. They are taught to follow routines, such as a bedtime routine and classroom routines before they become really skillful at organizing their own time and priorities. Teaching students to utilize external organizational systems and establishing specific organizational routines are the essential first steps in addressing Executive Functioning Skills.

Zones, or areas where specific activities occur, labels and containers are types of external systems that can be put into place to assist students with learning and organization. Visual parameters establish clear boundaries to show where the area starts and where it ends. Having only the materials needed for a specific task or activity present helps to limit distractions and assist with efficiency. By having *zones* established and teaching students to set up their own *zones*, it is possible to promote independence and efficiency.

| Unit 2: Lesson 1 | **Lesson 1:** Organizing Space |

Materials

- CLUSTER ORGANIZERS (ROPES 01, 02, 03)
- TASK/CHECKLISTS (ROPES 05-05, 05-10, 05-15)
- VENN DIAGRAM (ROPES 11)

Lesson 1-Activity 1: *Identifying Organizational Supports*
Set Up

Prior to this activity, the teacher must establish 6-8 *specific visual and organizational supports* and identified areas in the classroom. Ensure that these are clearly structured and identifiable areas. Examples of locations where specific visual and organizational supports would be needed include but are not limited the following:

- Where homework is turned in
- Where assignments are listed on board
- What the daily schedule of events will be
- What the behavioral rules and expectations are
- Where student materials are (pencils, paper, books, etc.)
- Where the student computer is, etc.

Prior to beginning this activity, have the "name" of each area written on an index card.

Steps for Participation

1. Explain that in this lesson students will learn how to identify various visual information and environmental structures that are in place to help them get organized and to help them to understand the different expectations in various places.

   a. Explain how the environment gives us information to help us plan and get organized. It tells us what we should do and where tasks should occur.

2. List on the board and discuss the various visual information and structure the students encounter at the mall, amusement parks, grocery stores, movie theaters and libraries, etc.

   a. In these examples ask students to share which information in the environment "tells" them what to do and where to go.

   b. Examples include maps, signs, arrows, words, placement of objects (benches, cash registers, grocery carts, bins, boxes, lights, labels), employee uniforms, schedules (hours of operation, movie schedules, bus schedules), etc.

   c. Have the students share examples with details from their personal experiences.

   d. Spend time discussing and sharing the cues and clues in these settings.

3. Ask students to explain how they would know where to go and what to do if this information was not there.

   a. Ask them what they do to "figure out" where to go and what to do if they were going to a "new" or novel place they had never been to before.

4. Then, arrange students in teams and give each team one of the prepared index cards with a label specific to the classroom areas that were arranged.

   a. Have the teams match the card to each area in the classroom.

   b. Then, ask students to explain how they "knew" the purpose of each area and ask what each area tells them.

   c. For example, one label might read "Student Information Area" which includes the class schedule, rules, and homework assignments, which is information initiated by the teacher to communicate expectations.

d. Another example is the "Student Materials Area" which has paper, pencils, rules, reference books. Another might read "Student Computer Area" which has student sized chairs and monitors.

5. Explain that often locations serve multiple purposes. In these cases people need to look for additional visual information to help tell them the different expectations at that time.

   a. For example, the *Gym* could be used for a volleyball game, a basketball game or a dance.

   b. Ask students to explain how they would know which purpose the gym was being used for by describing the things that they might see.

   c. Emphasize that the environment, including visual and physical structures, gives us information about what to do and what to expect and by changing this information, it changes the message and expectations.

6. Explain that in the classroom a student desk could have multiple purposes.

   a. At one part of the day it could be used as part of the larger group learning activity and a different part of the day it could be used for independent student work.

   b. Ask students how they know the difference.

   c. Ask how the desk placement implies different expectations: compare whether desks are in a group facing one another or spread apart. How are the expectations different?

   d. Spend time discussing this with the students.

   e. Their participation is important for getting them to "understand" their surroundings.

7. Explain that the location of the teacher in the classroom could imply different expectations.

   a. Ask students to describe how the location of the teacher tells the students what the expectations are.

   b. Ask how the expectations differ if the teacher is in front of the group talking versus sitting at the teacher desk.

8. Explain that in school, the environment is usually set up and structured to help students know what to do and to support their organization. However, there will be many situations they encounter where these supports will not automatically be in place.

a. Students will have to learn to put in place their own set of environmental supports and structures to assist themselves with organization.

9. Lead a class activity and have the students identify one good and one poor example of visual information and structure that occurs naturally on the school campus.

   a. Examples could include the library, cafeteria, front office, various classrooms, Gym, etc.

   b. Have students discuss and share the strengths and weaknesses of these examples with the group.

10. Ask students to provide ideas for visual supports and structures that could be *added* to improve their examples of poor organizational structure on campus.

11. Be prepared with a specific example to get students going in the right direction with this activity.

    a. For example, ask students if in the front office, is it "clear" which secretary is the main one who can answer questions, etc.

Lesson 1-Activity 2: *Creating Organizational Supports using Labeled Containers and Task Boxes*

Materials

- White board and markers
- CLUSTER ORGANIZER (ROPES 01, 02, 03)
- TASK/CHECKLISTS (ROPES 05-05, 05-10, 05-15)

Set Up

Have a list of real life examples of containers used for organizing specific tasks or materials: utensil drawer, dresser with clothes, fishing tackle box, tool box, homework in-box, binders (math, language arts, science), backpack, purse, gym bag, make-up, etc. Show several concrete examples of containers to organize your materials. Have a place for everything. Examples could include pen holder, paper clip holder, trays, wallet, lunch box, briefcase, etc.

1. Draw a CLUSTER ORGANIZER on the board with "Ways Labeled Containers Help" in the center circle.

2. In the outer circles write several reasons labeled containers help.

3. Draw another cluster on the board, in the center circle of this CLUSTER ORGANIZER write, "Containers Used by Successful Students."

4. In the outer circles write the students' ideas, including binders and folders in backpacks (show examples), student supply boxes (with pencils, erasers, whiteout, pens, highlighters, and paperclips), locker shelves, lunch box, student planners, etc.

5. Discuss the value of using labeled containers and point out how common these are in our daily lives.

   a. Point out examples in the grocery store, clothing stores, sporting goods stores (hangers, baskets, shelves, etc.)

Lesson 1-Activity 3: *Creating Student Supply Boxes*

Materials

- CLUSTER ORGANIZER (ROPES 01, 02, 03)
- TASK/CHECKLISTS (ROPES 05-05, 05-10, 05-15)

Set Up

The teacher should have an idea of the needed materials required by each student's teacher. This will take communication and planning with the General Education Teachers, but it is essential for student success.

The teacher should have materials for student supply boxes purchased, sorted into labeled containers and available *prior* to this activity. If the School District does not plan to provide these materials, then students should obtain them from home. These are essential materials to student success and are not optional.

Suggested Student Supplies: 3 x 5 cards, pencils, erasers, post-it notes, paper clips, sharpeners, highlighters, whiteout, mini stapler, storage container, pens, etc. Consult with the General Education teachers for specific supplies required for classes.

Step for Participation

1. Draw a CLUSTER ORGANIZER on board with "Student Supply Box" in the center circle.

2. Have students brainstorm the items that are needed in the supply boxes and record these in the outer circles. See samples listed under materials.

3. Ask students to access their lists that were provided by their teachers (if available) to help generate ideas.

4. After brainstorming is complete, have students create a "Student Supply Box CHECKLIST" on a 3 x 5 index card.

    a. The teacher should collect these cards and laminate them for students to keep in their binders.

5. The next day the teacher should have all items needed for student supply boxes available in the classroom or assign as homework if supplies are not going to be provided by the school.

    a. Students will take their lists and use them to fill their supply box.

6. After filling their boxes, have students work with a partner to "check off" all items on their lists that are now in their supply boxes.

    a. The "check-off" process is important to staying organized and tracking progress.

    b. Be prepared to discuss this simple yet important aspect of CHECKLISTS.

7. The teacher should explain to students that this box is a tool to use across the school day, it should be kept in their backpacks and used as needed.

    a. Explain that successful students keep needed materials ready and accessible at all times.

    b. Encourage the students as they adopt these new skills.

8. Once per week, there should be a scheduled organizational routine when students should restock their supply boxes.

    a. The students may earn points for having an organized, well stocked student supply box when the teacher conducts these periodic checks.

Lesson 1-Activity 4: *Creating Student Binders*

Materials

- A 2-3 inch binder for each student (or a 1-2 inch colored binder for each subject area)
- Colored tabbed dividers with pockets for each student
  - This will vary based on the number of subjects
- Color coded homework folders for each student
- 5 sheet protectors for each student
- Colored book covers to coordinate with each colored tab divider or subject binder
- Labels for binders and tab dividers

- CLUSTER ORGANIZER (ROPES 01, 02, 03)
- TASK/CHECKLISTS (ROPES 05-05, 05-10, 05-15) or 3 x 5 index cards for each student

Set Up

Each student must have a binder and all the materials listed above to learn to be organized. If the School District does not supply the materials for the student binders, it would be necessary to assign this as homework. Managing a student binder is a critical component of the class and one of the core organization deficits that impacts student success. This activity is not optional. It must be a part of the regular class routines and practices.

The teacher should plan to have all necessary organizational materials available in advance, organized in labeled containers so students can construct their binders.

NOTE: The teacher will have to create a Binder Construction CHECKLIST in advance for the steps on *how to* construct the binder and then record it on the board in Step 9.

Step for Participation

1. Create a CLUSTER ORGANIZER on the board and write in the center circle, "Materials needed to Organize School Work."
2. Ask the students to share the ways in which they currently organize their schoolwork.
3. List student responses in the outer circles of the CLUSTER ORGANIZER.
   a. If no organizational structures exists then be prepared to ask students for reasons why they don't exist.
   b. The outer circles may include: folders, blank paper, notes, class schedule, dividers, pockets, labels, sheet protectors, colored book covers, etc.
4. Ask students how each item in the outer circles helps them to stay organized.
   a. This could be a challenge for students to explain so be prepared to prompt answers if needed.
   b. Example: Dividers help to know where each subject begins and ends, folders help to identify work to be done and work to do, book covers help to identify specific subjects.
   c. Explain that it is important that students understand the reasons these tools are used and the function/purpose of each.

    d. Students struggle with understanding how essential materials help them to stay organized. They can be told to use these strategies, but they need to understand why they are useful if they are to incorporate them into independent daily use.

5. After the CLUSTER ORGANIZER is filled with essential student materials, transfer the list of items to a master CHECKLIST of essential student materials on the board.

6. Then, have students record the essential items, from the board CHECKLIST for their student binders, on a personal CHECKLIST.

    a. The personal CHECKLISTS should be kept in the folder for future reference.

    b. NOTE: The teacher should have items organized and labeled in advance in the classroom or should have assigned the students to bring items needed for their student binders so the students can construct their student binders during the next class period.

7. Using the students' personal essential materials CHECKLISTS have the students gather items to complete their own student binders.

    a. They should check off each item on their CHECKLIST as they get it.

    b. If this is not practical then have the students take the materials to their desks and check them off at their desks.

    c. The check off aspect of the list is important to help them stay organized.

8. After students have gathered items have them construct their binders as a group.

    a. NOTE: Have a sample binder made up in advance for students to view.

9. Write the teacher created Binder Construction CHECKLIST from Set Up on the board. (See NOTE in Set Up above.)

    a. The binder construction CHECKLIST will look unique for each teacher.

    b. A sample Binder Construction CHECKLIST might include:

       i. Take one label and attach it to the front of the blue homework folder.

      ii. Write Math Homework on the label.

       iii. Inside the blue folder, adhere a label on the left side that says "to do" on the right side of the blue folder adhere a label that says "done."

   c. Each step of the binder will have to be detailed in this way.

   d. Be prepared for how the binders will look.

   e. This will take time and planning in advance.

10. As students construct their binders, have them identify the purpose of each element in the binder so they understand what each element does for them to help keep them organized.

11. The teacher should model how to use the student binder to stay organized each day.

   a. Students should earn class points for completing the binder organization routine each week.

   b. Random binder/backpack checks could be conducted for class reward points or extra credit.

Lesson 1-Activity 5: *Organizing Backpacks*

Materials
- CHECKLISTS (ROPES 01, 02, 03)
- VENN DIAGRAM (ROPES 11)

Set Up

Put a VENN DIAGRAM on the board. Ask the students to have their backpack at their desks. NOTE: If students are reluctant to volunteer or as an alternative, the teacher can have two "contrived" student backpacks to use for demonstration purposes. One set up to represent an "organized" backpack, the other one set up to represent a "disorganized" backpack.

Steps for Participation

1. Ask an organized student to dump the backpack out so the contents can be compared to a messy backpack.

   a. Record the items on the *left side* of the VENN DIAGRAM labeled "organized."

2. Ask a student with a messy backpack, perhaps someone who struggles with organizational skills, to dump the contents of the backpack.

   a. Record the items on the *right side* of the VENN DIAGRAM labeled "messy."

3. Discuss each item in the VENN DIAGRAM and have students evaluate whether each is an *important item* to have in a well-organized student backpack or not.

   a. Move all of the "essential backpack items" to the *middle section* of the VENN DIAGRAM.

   b. Discuss the concept that a clean backpack only has the "essential items."

4. Using a CHECKLIST or a 3x5 card, have students create a "clean backpack" CHECKLIST with all of the essential items listed in the center of the VENN DIAGRAM.

   a. This CHECKLIST should be laminated and kept in the student binder.

   b. The list will be used as part of a "backpack organizational routine" which will take place weekly on a specific day the teacher determines in advance.

   c. NOTE: This list should include their student supply boxes, text books and student binders created in previous lessons.

Lesson 1- Activity 6: *Sorting and Purging Backpacks*

Materials

- CHECKLIST (ROPES 05-05, 05-10, 05-10)

Set Up

Each student will need three bins or three different colored standard size pieces of paper. Have a sample backpack prepared in advance or ask for a student volunteer to provide one. The sample backpack should have *essential* and *nonessential* items in it.

1. Place three bins or papers on the table and have students label them as follows: Give Away, Throw Away, and Put Away.

2. Empty the contents of the sample backpack on the table.

3. Discuss *each item* from the backpack

4. Demonstrate what to do with each of the items found in the student backpacks:

   a. *Give Away:* Turn in to teacher, return to the owner, take home to parent or take home permanently

   b. *Throw Away:* These are items the student is completely finished with that are trash or recycling

     c. *Put Away:* These are items that need to be kept or filed in the student binder to be held onto while you are completing them or using them.

5. After viewing the demonstration with the sample backpack, have students go through the items in their backpacks and place each item in the correct pile or bin.

6. IMPORTANT NOTE: Regarding the *"Throw Away"* pile, often students think that things are trash when actually they are items that should be held onto for a while longer.

     a. Examples are notes that have been taken in class or assignments that have been returned to a student with a grade on them. They may think they are finished with these items, but they may come in handy when studying for a final or later test. Explain to student that when in doubt– file it!

7. Show students how to file the items in the "Put Away" pile into their student binders using appropriate organizational structures and strategies.

8. Using the clean backpack CHECKLIST from the previous activity, have the students return only the *"essential items"* listed on their CHECKLISTS to the backpacks.

9. As part of a weekly organizational routine, students should use the clean backpack CHECKLIST.

     a. Their work should be checked for class points.

     b. Random clean backpack checks could be conducted for class reward points or extra credit.

Unit 2: Lesson 2 | **Lesson 2: Organizing Time**

Content Information for Teachers

Often it is difficult for students to shift their attention from one activity to another, particularly when they are engaging in an activity that does not have automatic closure. Timers are one strategy for assisting with this issue. For example, it is fairly clear when to stop unloading the dishwasher, when all the dishes are put away, but when should one stop watching You Tube videos? It is fairly clear when the math homework is done because all of the problems on the page are solved, but when do you stop reading the 350 page novel? Timers with programmable alarms can indicate when to stop *"open-ended"* assignments such as reading or studying.

Materials

Teachers will need to have a variety of timers with alarms to show students for this activity. Timers which have both a visual and auditory component can extremely helpful.

- Time Timer® (www.timetimer.com). This is a visual timer that counts down and shows how much time is remaining with numbers and a strip of red. When the red is gone and the timer arm reaches 0, the time is up. It is also available as an app for mobile devices.

- Cell phones or tablets with alarm reminder functions

Lesson 2-Activity 1: *Identifying "Opened-Ended" Activities*

Set Up

The teacher should put a list of activities on the board, many of which are *"close-ended"* and many of which are *"open-ended"* and may require a time limit to signal the end point. Examples of *"open-ended"* activities include: studying, reading, listening to music, studying, playing X-box, watching You Tube, watering the garden, etc. Examples of close ended activities include: doing a worksheet with a specific number of problems, writing vocabulary words five times each, unloading the dishwasher, folding a basket of laundry, etc. Be prepared with 20 various activities to demonstrate this lesson.

Steps for Participation

1. Ask students to look at the list of activities on the board and determine which ones are *"open-ended"* and may need to have a time limit on them and which ones have automatic finishing points.

2. Discuss how this can be determined and when an activity could be *"open-ended"* or closed for example, reading five pages vs. reading until you are finished with the entire book vs. reading for 30 minutes.

3. Explain to students that *"open-ended"* activities can be hard to manage because we may not know when to shift away from them and move on to something else.

4. Ask students to identify strategies that may help with *shifting*, stopping one activity and refocusing on a different activity, from these *"open-ended"* activities.

5. Ask students to identify strategies including setting a specific time to shift, number of minutes to do the activity or imposing a limit on the number of pages produced.

6. Ask the students to identify visual supports that can assist with shifting attention.

   a. Prompt students to identify book marks or post-it notes that mark the shifting point of a task or timers and that can signal the *end* of the time limit for the activity.

7. In Class or as Homework: Ask students to practice identifying open-ended activities that they encounter in their daily lives. This may be especially important related to high preference activities, since these are often the most challenging activities for students to end.

Lesson 2-Activity 2: *Using Alarms and Timers in "Opened-Ended" Tasks*

Set Up

Set up a schedule with 3-4 *"open-ended"* activities and write the sequence on the board. These can be silly or serious. For example, open book and read; put head on desk to rest your eyes; talk about your weekend with a friend; watch your favorite videos on You Tube, etc.

Steps for Participation

1. Have students read the posted schedule to review each task with the group.

2. Ask students to identify which activities are "open-ended" and how they might set up a schedule to impose some closure on the "open-ended" tasks.

3. Show the students the timer and ask them when they have used one in their lives (e.g. cooking).

4. Explain that the timer will serve as the *signal* for them to shift to the next activity on the schedule.

5. Set the timer for the predetermined amount of time and remind the students that when the timer expires, as indicated by the auditory cue, or in the case of the Time Timer, when the red is gone, the students *must stop* what they are doing, check the schedule, and move on to the next activity.

   a. NOTE: Initially the teacher will set the timer, the students will eventually be responsible for this step.

6. Once the timer has expired, wait to see if the students remember what to do. If they successfully stop the cur-

rent activity and move onto the next, provide them with Reward Points.

7. If students stop the activity, but do not move onto the next one, use an indirect verbal cue such as,

    a. "What should you do now that _____ is finished?"

    b. If they still do not know, provide a more direct verbal cue such as, "Where do you need to look to find the answer?"

    c. If they still do not respond, give a directive such as, "check the schedule."

8. If the timer expires and the students do not stop the initial activity, approach them with the timer and provide an indirect prompt such as tapping the timer and giving an expectant look.

9. If needed, provide increasingly direct cues such as,

    a. "Look, the time has expired, what does that mean?" "What do you need to do now?"

    b. If necessary, review the timer procedure completely with the students and then give a direct instruction to "stop" the activity and go on to the next.

10. If students stop and then transition to the next activity, provide additional Reward Points.

11. The eventual goal is for the students to independently impose a limit on *"opened-ended"* tasks, set the timer, do the task and then stop the task once the time has expired and move on to the next activity as indicated, without requiring additional prompts or cues from another person.

    a. NOTE: This is a process and will take time for the students to learn. Continue to use timers throughout all instructional activities as much as possible.

Lesson 2-Activity 3: *Using Timers to Limit Preferred Activities*

Materials

- Time Timer ® or a timer with a visual and auditory indicator
- Students can use their own electronic devices (e.g., iPod, iPad, cell phone) for this activity

Set Up

Some students have difficulty limiting highly *preferred* activities, passions and interests. A timer is a necessity when teaching students to limit their time. It can be used to remind students of how long it is until they are allowed the highly preferred activity, even if the activity is doing nothing in particular. It can be used to remind students how much time is left to enjoy the highly preferred activity before shifting back to a less preferred activity. Additional strategies will be discussed within procedures for teaching self-management of behaviors in future units.

Steps for Participation

1. Have each student pick one preferred activity that will be done in the classroom setting such as listening to music, drawing, reading, playing a game, etc.

2. Explain that students can choose a preferred activity of their choice, but when the timer rings all students must stop the preferred activity and put their heads on the desk with their eyes closed.

3. Explain that the timer will be set for five minutes and then it will ring.

   a. If a Time Timer® is used then explain that the red indicator will let students know the time left is decreasing.

   b. Explain that when the timer rings, the expectation is for the students to "stop" the current activity and put their heads down on the desk with their eyes closed, even if they do not perceive the activity to be finished.

4. Once the timer has expired, wait to see if the students remember what to do. If they successfully stop the current activity and put their heads down, provide them with Reward Points.

5. If students stop the activity, but do not put their heads on the desk, use an indirect verbal cue such as, "What should you do now that the timer has rung?"

   a. If they still do not know, provide a more direct verbal cue such as, "Remember what to do at your desks?"

   b. If they still do not respond, give a directive such as, "Stop the activity and put your heads on the desk."

6. *Repeat the activity above and this time have the students "stop" the current activity and "look" at the teacher for additional information and instruction.*

7. Be prepared to give feedback to students on how they responded when the timer went off (see above steps).

8. Ask students to identify which activities could be limited in their own lives (e.g., video games, computer time, watching TV, socializing).

9. Ask students to identify reasons they would use a timer to limit activities (e.g., keeping track of time, getting important things done).

10. Homework Activity

    a. Have students use a timer at home to assist with limiting a specific predetermined preferred activity (watching TV, playing a game, reading, talking on the phone, listening to music, etc.).

    b. Have students report back to the class which task they used a timer with and how they used it.

Lesson 3: Organizing Work: Reminder Boards, Calendars, Schedules

Materials

- CHECKLISTS (ROPES 05-05, 05-10, 05-15)
- MONTHLY PLANNING CALENDAR (ROPES-08)
- DAILY SCHEDULE (ROPES-09)
- Post-it notes
- Mini notebook
- Reminder board

Lesson 3-Activity 1: *Using Reminder Boards/Pages and "Notes to Self"*

Materials

- Post-it notes

Set Up

Have a reminder board set up in the classroom. Use it *frequently* to remind students of upcoming events or changes in routine. When it is used point out to the students the how and why functions of the board. Examples: Remember minimum day on Friday, Remember Permission Slips Due Tuesday, Assembly on Thursday, etc. When appropriate, remind students to use their personal reminder page or "notes-to-self page" in their student binders or on their tablets/cell phones. Try to use indirect prompts, such as "This seems important. What could help us all remember this?" Try to avoid giving direct instructions.

Step for Participation

1. Assign a *designated reminder page* or "note-to-self" in the student binder or on their tablets/cell phones and inform

students that this is a place to keep reminder notes about important projects, events, timelines, activities, needed materials, etc.

   a. Students should be taught to add items to their reminder pages on a daily basis.

2. Provide students with Post-it notes or appropriate writing instruments for making reminder notes or instruct them on how to use the appropriate app on their tablets/phones.

3. When there is an important event for students to remember or to add to their daily schedule, remind them to write a "reminder note" and place it in the designated location. Reward Points may be given when students make reminder Independently initiated reminder earn Reward Points.

4. Draw a CLUSTER ORGANIZER on the board.

   a. In the center circle write "common things students forget."

5. Have students generate ideas of things that they commonly forget to do and write these in the outer circles.

   a. For example, take PE clothes home on Friday to be washed, bring back permission slip or money for field trip, etc.

6. NOTE: When conducting daily or weekly student binder checks, ask students to describe any items they should put on their "notes-to-self page or app"

   a. Give Reward Points for appropriate use of this page or app by students.

   b. Reward the use of the system! The students should be rewarded for independently putting items on the reminder page or "note-to-self", even if later the reminders are not relevant.

   c. Some training can be done to assist students with determining relevant vs. irrelevant reminders.

Lesson 3-Activity 2: *Using Monthly Calendars*

Materials

- MONTHLY PLANNING CALENDAR (ROPES-08)

Content Information for Teachers

The monthly calendar is used to show when regularly occurring and irregularly occurring monthly and weekly events will take place. At this point, introduce the monthly calendar by showing students how to schedule regularly occurring and irregularly occurring routines for the month. This will help them to begin long-term planning and simple adjustments that are necessary in the time management process. In the coming units, the monthly calendar will also be used as a tool to teach management of complex tasks, assignments, and projects as well as setting goals and managing priorities.

Set Up

Have a large monthly calendar posted on the classroom wall to show students how and when to use this strategy. Demonstrate how you use a monthly calendar to give assignments, make appointments, schedule events, etc. Model its use daily as part of the daily routine for this class.

For this activity be prepared with a list of 8-10 activities and assignments posted on the board. The students will transfer these activities and assignments onto their personal calendars for *practice* (details below). Following the practice, have the students create a "real" monthly calendar with real assignment due dates, project dates and school wide activities. Gathering this information from the school office and teachers will take planning. The students may need to ask their teachers for a monthly assignment list to bring to the Study Skills Class. This will allow the study skills teacher to assist them in completing the MONTHLY PLANNING CALENDAR with their actual assignments .

Steps for Participation

Explain to students that the monthly calendar will help them better manage their time by helping them plan for long-term goals and activities.

Use the white board or overhead to demonstrate how to fill in the calendar.

1. Using the sample on the board, model how to record the regularly scheduled weekly and monthly activities such as: soccer practice, soccer games, karate practice, spelling tests, etc.

2. Next, give students their own practice monthly calendar template.

    a. Have them record the regularly scheduled events onto their practice calendar.

3. Have a list of 4-5 made up special events or activities on the board. Make them silly like, bring your dog to school day.

    a. Have the students transfer the special events onto their practice calendar.

4. Have a list of 4-5 due dates for school work/assignments listed on the board and have students practice recording them on their practice calendar.

5. Next, give them a blank calendar to complete with "real" regularly scheduled activities, assignments, special events, etc.

    a. Demonstrate how to use the monthly calendar to record due dates for long term projects or major tests. You may need to get this in advance from teachers.

    b. The students will learn, as described in the coming chapters, how to break long-term projects down into components and plot out the "work time" required for completing the steps and meeting the deadlines, but at this point, simply recording the due dates will start the process.

6. NOTE: As stated in the "set up" details matter here, so the teacher should to be aware of the students' daily and monthly assignments and project dates.

    a. The point of this activity is to "teach students" how to organize their work using calendars.

    b. This is a long term process and probably one that they have not yet been properly taught to do.

7. Next, have students fill in any irregular routines or activities that are scheduled for that month. These can include special events or activities like spirit week, minimum days, unit or chapter tests, dances, field trips, club meetings, athletic contests, etc.

8. Explain that often irregular events come up that may conflict with events already on the calendar. When this happens it is called a "Schedule Conflict" and something needs to happen to adjust the calendar to accommodate the new event.

9. Demonstrate for the students a "Schedule Conflict" and how it can be resolved, for example:

    a. Moving one activity to another day/time or postponing an activity to a later date, etc.

    b. Show how a family trip to the beach scheduled for September 5th conflicted with the regular Saturday soccer routine.

        i. In this case, the trip could be postponed until the following weekend or the soccer game was rescheduled or forfeited.

10. Initially, the teachers should simply point out the potential for or real schedule conflict to the students and show them how to make the necessary adjustments to their calendars to accommodate these issues. In the units that follow, the skills necessary for making and adjusting the schedule will be taught.

11. NOTE: The process for filling in the monthly calendar should be repeated at the beginning of every month throughout the school year.

   a. Ensure that each student's individual monthly planning calendar is kept in a convenient location at the front of the students' binders and/or is easily accessible on their tablet/computer or cell phone.

   b. The calendars will be reviewed during daily and weekly check-ins.

Lesson 3-Activity 4: *Using a Class Schedule*

Materials

- DAILY SCHEDULE (ROPES 09)
- WORK PLAN FORM

Steps for Participation

1. Post a daily schedule for the class on the white board and follow it every day.

   a. A daily schedule should be used to show what the students will be doing that day and in what order the activities will occur.

   b. The schedule should be made and revised each day based on the priorities for that day and the time estimated for each activity.

2. The teacher should demonstrate checking off each activity as it is done.

   · Sample daily schedule might be: Copy homework into planner, complete a work plan with staff, participate in EF lesson, complete work on work plan, free/choice time, binder check, self-score class participation points, and put binder in backpack/pack up.

3. NOTE: It will be good to schedule in free/choice time a couple of times per week so that students can learn how to make appropriate choices during free time (see next section).

4. Have students copy the daily class schedule onto a blank schedule CHECKLIST form. Have the students read each ac-

tivity in the class and check off each activity on their personal schedule once the group has completed the activity.

5. Repeat the daily study skills class schedule activity for several days until students are using it without reminders. Class Reward Points may be earned for consistent use of the class schedule.

Lesson 3-Activity 5: *Free Time/Choice Time vs Work Time*

Steps for Participation

1. Create a T CHART on the board. On the left side write "Choice Activities." On the right side write "Work Activities"

2. Ask the students to generate lists of each, referring to "choice activities" that they can do in this class and "work activities" that they can do in this class.

3. Point out to students that each of them may have their own preferences and what they chose to do during their free time is their "choice".

4. Ask students how they decide when to do things on the "Work" side and when to do things on the "Choice" side.

   a. Guide them in recognizing that "Time/Due Dates" and "Bonus" or "Penalty" for doing or not doing the work are important considerations.

   b. NOTE: Prioritization will be covered in depth in Unit 7 Time Management. Introducing the vocabulary at this point will be helpful in preparation for upcoming Units.

5. Discuss with students that it is often necessary to give up some "free time" so that a critical task can be completed on time. Point out that "free time" is often eaten up when students are disorganized, do not make plans or do not finish tasks in a timely manner because of distractions, etc.

Unit 2: Lesson 4   **Lesson 4: Using Homework Management Systems and Planners**

Materials

- Colored folders with two pockets
- Labels
- HOMEWORK SUMMARY PAGE (ROPES 06)
- HOMEWORK SUMMARY PAGE (ROPES 07) or:
- School adopted planner, which may require additions or modifications for some students

- Use of an app or program for homework management such as istudiezpro, studious, etc.

Content Information for Teachers

In order to assist students with learning how to organize themselves, it is critical that teachers present information in a consistent and meaningful way. To assist with homework management, it is very helpful for teachers to write down all homework assignments on the board in a specific place, order and format each day or to consistently use the school management system, such as web based programs where teachers record homework assignments, grades, etc. If this is not occurring on your campus, it might be worth discussing at staff meetings and with administration. It might also be critical to write it into student IEPs as a necessary accommodation based on this identified area of need.

The consistent use of visual methods to indicate work expectations makes the information concrete. This increases the likelihood that students with EF challenges will attend to the information and use it more regularly.

It will be important to use or develop a campus wide system to access information for students on your caseload regarding daily and long term homework assignments, tests and projects. If these systems are not in place or being used regularly at your school site, you may have to establish another method for getting this information from all of the teachers on campus. It is critical that the study skills teacher is able to access information about students' work *prior* to deadlines as a means to prevent incomplete work and teach good study skills. Ultimately, work completion is the students' responsibility, but the point of this class is to teach students' better habits and replace ineffective student behaviors with successful student skills and habits. This ongoing process includes teaching accountability for school assignments and management of grades.

If study skills teachers have access to assignments in advance, they can teach the skills to students to pro-actively complete the work. Often, the ineffective strategy that is taught is for students to look for and complete LATE work for either full or partial credit. If this is the method being use on your campus, think about what is being taught.... Students learn to wait for the late assignments to be posted or reported to them, they then complete them for partial (or full credit), thus teaching them to be late, procrastinate and to wait for teachers to tell them what is missing. These are not good habits or expectations to establish if you think about the long term implications. Who is going to tell them what work is late/missing in college when they do not have an IEP or study skills class? What are the consequences for consistently being late on assignments in your career? The point of study skills is to learn "better" ways of organizing their work. The emphasis should be on learning these skills rather than just "getting the grades in the other classes." Passing the classes that they are enrolled in is critical, but it should not be the primary goal. Learning the life skills to succeed in post-secondary education and employment are the primary goals.

Lesson 4-Activity 1: *Using Homework Folders*

Materials

- Labels
- Two-pocket colored folders for each student, also called homework folders (color coded for each subject area)
    - A homework folder is a simple tool that indicates what needs to be done and how much there is to do.
    - It has a specific place to store assignments and materials and a way to indicate when the work is finished to ensure that students will complete all assignments and turn them in.
    - Using a left to right format with a "To Do" and "Finished" side to the folder is a simple way to keep homework, assignments and projects organized.
    - Using a simple written homework log assists students with managing both short and long term assignments.

Figure 2.1 Sample homework folder set up

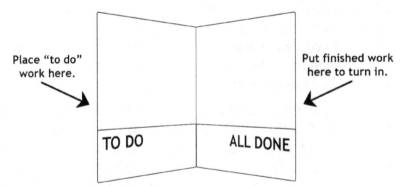

Place "to do" work here.   Put finished work here to turn in.

TO DO   ALL DONE

Steps for Participation

1. Generate 3-4 mock homework assignments and/or worksheets for students to complete during this activity.
2. Provide a folder and two labels for each student or use the folder developed in the binder system from a previous activity.

3. Have students construct the folder with the appropriate labels on each side.

   a. Have them put the incomplete worksheets and assignments on the left side labeled "To Do".

   b. Have the students complete the worksheets and put each worksheet in the "Finished Work" or "Done" pocket on the right side.

4. Students should be taught to put the new assignments and materials into the left side of the homework folder, the "to do" pocket, when they are assigned.

5. Once the work is done, students should be taught to put the completed work into the right pocket of the folder, the "finished" pocket.

6. Students should be taught to put the homework in the proper folder in their student binder and then put the binder in the backpack as soon as the work is assigned and/or completed.

7. NOTE: It recommended to meet with parents and teachers to explain this system or send them a written description so they can support and encourage its use.

8. NOTE: Have a system for checking in and monitoring each student's use of the homework system daily. Use Reward Points for success.

Lesson 4-Activity 2: *Using and Checking the Student Planner/Log*

Steps for Participation

1. Post homework assignments on the board in the Homework Summary Area.

   a. Write the information on the board in an organized way or teach students to use the online management system established by your school site or district administration.

   b. NOTE: Use this ONLY if it is a reliable source of information that is updated by all teachers regularly.

2. Include: Subject, Date Assigned, Assignment/Pages, Due Date and Materials needed to complete the assignment.

3. It is important for all General Education Teachers to agree to use a similar format for presenting homework assignments to student (e.g. writing them in a specific place on the board).

   a. This will take planning and coordination.

   b. The hope is that General Education Teachers will agree to post homework and project information in a designated area and format in their classrooms to assist students in learning this skill.

    c. This consistency can be a part of your school sites Universal Design for Learning (UDL), or Tier 1 interventions using multi-tiered systems of support.

4. Give students a blank HOMEWORK SUMMARY FORM or Student Planner.

    a. Students should be taught how to write down assignments and the materials needed on the summary sheet or in the student planner.

    b. Demonstrate this process creating a blank template on the board. Transfer information from the Homework Summary Area, on the wall or board, onto the HOMEWORK SUMMARY FORM or Student Planner.

    c. Example: Subject: Spelling, Date Assigned: Sept 1, 2012, Assignment: page 345 in Dictionary, write third word down on lined paper, due: tomorrow Sept 2, 2012. Materials: Dictionary

5. Next, have the students practice transferring the posted information from the board onto the HOMEWORK SUMMARY PAGE or Student Planner.

    a. Have students practice checking off completed assignments.

    b. Teach them to put completed work in their homework folder for that subject area to establish the practice of putting completed assignments in the designated binder spot.

    c. Use post-it notes to help remind students to get additional information from their teachers to keep the homework logs current and complete.

6. Students should be given daily feedback on their use of the homework summary system.

    a. This can be done during a daily check in/out procedure where planner checks, binder checks and work plans are completed.

    b. Class points should be provided for completing the student planner each day, for completing work on the work plan and for keeping the binder and backpack organized.

7. It is recommended that the teacher has a method for tracking the students' use of HOMEWORK SUMMARY SHEETS on a daily basis.

a. A chart on the wall with the students' names and dates is an easy and visual method.

b. If the summary sheet/planner is accurate and complete then a star could be recorded in the box.

c. This is a visual method for seeing progress and the increased use of a new skill.

d. Another method is to include *Planner Use* as part of the daily point summary that is being conducted at the end of each class session.

8. NOTE: It may be helpful to meet with the students' teachers to identify *a peer mentor* in each class to assist in accurately completing the planner during class time.

9. NOTE: It could be helpful to meet with parents to explain this system so they can support and encourage its use at home.

Figure 2.2 Sample of Basic Homework Summary

Subject	Date Assigned	Assignment	Due	Materials
Math	Monday Jan 21	Pgs. 21-22 odd problems	Tues. Jan 22	**Math book**
Spelling	Monday Jan 21	Study for test	Fri. Jan 25	**Spelling list & flashcards**
Science	Monday Jan 21	Volcano Project for Science Fair	Fri. Feb 25	**Card board, paper mache, red paint, brown paint**

Notes:

Unit 3: Evaluating Actions and Outcomes

Objectives

- Students will learn strategies to evaluate actions and choices in order to make good decisions with positive outcomes.

- Students will learn to predict outcomes in novel and familiar situations and then choose appropriate actions that result in positive or desirable outcomes.

- Students will also learn a process to reflect on behaviors that interfere with school or social success.

Content Information for Teachers

The relationship between actions and outcomes is difficult for many students to understand because they do not see the relationship between their "behaviors" and the outcomes or "consequences" that they experience. By providing a visual and graphic representation of this continuum applied to the students' real world experiences, the organizational thinking capacity can be developed, expanded and evaluated. The ability to think sequentially and relate situations to actions and actions to outcomes is a vital skill for choice making, self-evaluation, planning and goal setting. Using a graphic organizer that is frequently referred to as a "Thinking Tool", represented by a Circle, Square and Triangle gives students a visual representation of the relationship between a "Situation", their "Actions" and the "Outcome" resulting from their actions.

Lesson 1: Reflecting on Past Actions and Choices

Materials

- BASIC CRITICAL THINKING SKILLS WORKSHEET (ROPES-13). Also referred to as CST "Thinking Tool"

Lesson 1-Activity 1: *Evaluating "Good" Choices: "Daily Pat on the Back"*
Set Up

The CST "Thinking Tool" should always initially be presented from a positive perspective using the students' own real life experiences. This will help to establish the buy in of the students. It will also provide much needed positive self-reflection for the students as they develop these thinking skills. Once the initial understanding of the CST "Thinking Tool" is established and the students achieve an understanding that their actions have a direct relationship to the outcomes, then additional concepts can be taught using the CST "Thinking Tool". The *initial sequence of instruction* using the CST "Thinking Tool" uses a *backward chaining* method; starting with the triangle (outcome) then moving to the circle (behavior/ action), and finally completing the circle (situation/context).

Steps for Participation

1. Begin this activity by asking for a student volunteer to share an example of a positive personal accomplishment. Example might include learning a new trick on the skate-board or accomplishing a new personal best time in running the mile, making a sports team, etc.
2. Start by drawing a blank CST "Thinking Tool" on the board.
   a. Fill in the triangle with the positive accomplishment the student states.
3. Next, write in the square the actions, choices/specific physical behaviors, the student volunteer did to accomplish the positive outcome.
4. Finally, write in the circle the situation or circumstances that led to the actions that are written in the square.
5. The teacher should explain and define all vocabulary (situation, action, outcome and circle-square-triangle) during the activity.
   a. Lead a discussion on the meaning of situation, action, and outcome and other vocabulary that is often used to describe each.
      i. Situations: Context, Circumstances.
      ii. Actions: Behaviors, What you did, Steps, Action Plan.
      iii. Outcomes: Consequences, Goal, Accomplishment.
6. Once all three shapes are completed on the board, read back the sequence from the circle to the triangle, from left to right, describing the event back to the students.
   a. As the sequence is read write the words "situation" under the circle, "action" under the square, and "outcome" under the triangle.
7. After labeling the three components, draw in *arrows* showing the sequence of events from left to right.
   a. Discuss how the *circle* (situation) leads to the *square* (actions) which in turn leads to the outcome (triangle).
   b. The arrows are important as they demonstrate to the students that actions lead to outcomes or consequences.
8. Complete CST "Thinking Tool" as a group activity:
   a. Give each student a blank CST "Thinking Tool"

b. Ask students to identify something that they have done that they are proud of or something that they have accomplished, achieved or earned in the past.

c. Have the students record it in the triangle of the CST "Thinking Tool".

   i. This could be demonstrated again on the board to help students track and "see" the process using another example.

d. Ask the students to list what they did to make that positive *outcome* occur. Use vocabulary such as "What did you *do*? What were the *steps*? Or "What *actions* did you take?"

   i. Remember to teach the vocabulary throughout the activity, as necessary.

   ii. Settle on a term that seems to have the most power with the students.

e. Have the students record their actions in the square of the CST "Thinking Tool".

9. Ask the students to describe or define the situation (circle) or reason they took those actions.

a. This is the most challenging component of the process and often requires the most specific line of questioning.

b. Ask specific questions such as where, when, who, what did you need? In addition to asking the obvious, ask the most challenging question of "why did you do what you did? What was your reason or motivation?"

c. Have students record their answers in the *circle* of the CST "Thinking Tool".

10. Once all three components are completed on their form, select a student volunteer to read back the sequence they have written starting with the *circle* to the *triangle* reading from left to right.

11. As the student reads the sequence write it on the board.

a. As the sequence is read aloud write the words "situation" under the circle, "action" under the square, and "outcome" under the triangle.

b. Review the discussion on the meaning of situation, action, and outcome and other common vocabulary.

12. Next, with a different color pen draw arrows between the circle → square → triangle.

a. Review that the arrows are important as one event

"leads to" another.

    b. Emphasize the order of the sequence and highlight the direction that the arrows go (from left to right).

    c. Consequences and choices are not random actions that occur in a vacuum.

    d. Emphasize the direct relationship between what the students did and the positive outcome that resulted.

13. Congratulate the students on the accomplishment, then lead a discussion about the "choice" they made in their actions "square" relates to the outcome "triangle".

    a. Choice will be revisited and expanded on at a later point, but it is good to introduce the vocabulary now.

14. Have the students give themselves or each other, if doing this activity in a group, a "Pat on the Back" for a job well done!

15. Repeat this activity with multiple students and across several days, reflecting on past events that have had positive and good outcomes.

    a. Repeat the modeling of this activity until the students are able to accurately describe and provide details for each component of the CST "Thinking Tool" independently.

    b. Daily or frequent practice will not only help to develop this skill but will also provide an opportunity for positive self-reflection for students who may not have many positive experiences in their lives due to behavior or other learning related challenges.

Figure 3.1 Sample "Daily Pat on the Back"

The Basic "Thinking Tool"

Situation:

Teacher assigned a list of 20 words for the class to learn to spell. Test was scheduled for 1 week later.

Action:

I made flashcards and practiced them every night for 10 minutes.

Outcome:

I earned an A (20 out of 20) on the test. Mom let me rent a videogame on Friday.

Lesson 2: Choice Making

Content Information for Teachers

The concept of choice is difficult for students who lack organizational thinking. Many students simply get through the day by using rote or memorized procedures or routines, thus the notion of options and choice may be very foreign to them. In addition, without the ability to think forward about possible outcomes of their actions, many students simply go through the day reacting to the situations they encounter. To truly understand choice, students must be taught the "concept of choice" as it applies to their real world experiences. Again, it is critical to teach this concept framed first in the positive. Often we talk about bad choices as part of a lecture or consequence. To get student buy in with a deeper understanding of "choice" start by helping students reflect on the positive or good choices they make.

Lesson 2-Activity 1: *Making Good Choices*
Material

- BASIC CRITICAL THINKING SKILLS WORKSHEET (ROPES-13).

- GOALS WORKSHEET (ROPES-14): This is designed as a cluster organizer with *triangle* in center and *squares* in the outer area.

- EVALUATING and SELECTING APPROPRIATE ACTIONS (ROPES-20).

Set Up

Lead a discussion about prediction by showing students many concrete examples of how *Actions* lead to → *Outcomes.* Prepare a list of prediction ideas to use in a group activity. Suggested ideas might be:

- Square = water plant → triangle = plant lives
- Square = gas in the car → triangle = get to school
- Square = buy groceries → triangle = eat dinner
- Square = wash clothes → triangle = look good, presentable
- Square = pay bills → triangle = get electricity

Ask students to predict the outcome if the action did not happen for example, "action" is brush teeth daily which results in the "outcome" of clean teeth, fresh breath, no cavities; but if

55

action is did not brush teeth then the outcome: dirty teeth, bad breath and cavities.

In summary, the triangle in the CST "Thinking Tool" is the desired outcome or goal that the students want to achieve. The square is the action plan or steps the students must perform in order to obtain the outcome. The circle provides clarification about the timeline and setting conditions for performing the actions to obtain the goal, which are basically the reasons why a certain action plan and outcome is desired.

Steps for Participation

1. Discuss each scenario from the Set Up and write out the various actions (squares) and their corresponding outcomes (triangles) for both good and bad choices.

    a. Use the directional arrow to show the relationship is causal and that actions lead to outcomes in the examples.

2. Draw a CST "Thinking Tool" on the board

    a. In the circle write "teacher assigned 20 spelling words to study and will give a test one week later."

    b. In the square write, "made flashcards and studied for 10 minutes daily."

    c. In the triangle write, "got an A on the test."

3. Lead a discussion about good "choices." Ask the students "What if the student made a different choice?"

4. Below the positive action (square) from the samples, draw an empty square and record a different (less desirable) action.

    a. For example, if the action (square) was "doing my nightly math homework" on the original "CST Thinking Tool", write an alternative such as "Blow off math homework, play video games instead" in the alternative square underneath the positive action square.

5. On the board, draw a new, *blank triangle* under the original triangle and ask the students to "predict" what the outcome of this new action or choice would be. Ask students if they think the new outcome (new triangle) would be the same or different than it was in the original CST "Thinking Tool" sequence.

6. Ask students if they can predict what might happen (new triangle = outcome) if the student would have blown off the homework, rather than doing it.

    a. Record the possible outcomes in the new triangles as they are stated.

    b. Use the arrows to emphasize in both the positive and negative examples that it was the actions in squares that led to the outcomes in the triangles.

7. Using the diagram on the board, restate the original "good choice and outcome" followed by the made up "poor choice" and outcome and ask the students "Which was the good or better choice?"

    a. Use the directional arrows between the Circle, Square and Triangle to show the direction or sequence of events.

    b. The directional arrows continually remind the students of the "relationship" between actions (squares) and outcomes (triangles).

8. On the board, complete this process using 2 or 3 more examples until the students understand the connection between actions and outcomes.

9. Use the CST "Thinking Tool" to explain choice making by sketching choices and having the students identify possible outcomes in real world scenarios and contexts.

    a. Continue to use this same side by side comparison of "Good Choice" vs. "Poor Choice" on the board throughout future class periods.

    b. Provide Reward Points positive feedback and encouragement to the students for making good choices.

10. Next, in teams, have students come up with their own examples showing a good choice verses a bad choice using the CST "Thinking Tool".

    a. Have teams share the sequences with the group.

    b. Encourage students as they begin to "see" the relationship between their actions and outcomes.

11. Use this tool as often as possible within the class.

    a. Keep a diagram on the board or wall at all times.

    b. It is important to capture examples as they arise. For instance, in a social group if a student wants to listen to a certain song and another student wants to listen to something different, interrupt the activity and sketch a CST "Thinking Tool" with the options for solving the problem.

    c. Ask students based on the choices generated, which "choice" (square) might work best for both students (triangle/outcome). "Best" is defined as both people can live with outcome (triangle).

12. After this activity, consistently make a point to use the CST "Thinking Tool" regularly to practice good "choice making." Students need to be reminded that outcomes (triangles) whether positive or negative, usually result from choices (squares). This is a key theme that should be emphasized regularly.

Figure 3.2 Sample CST "Thinking Tool"

Predicting Outcomes and Choice Making

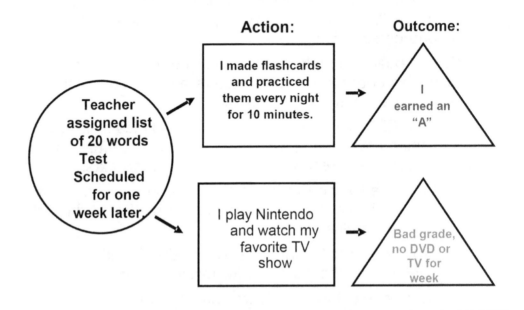

Lesson 3: Goal Setting

Content for Teachers

Setting short term personal goals is relatively easy to teach once the students have mastered the use of the CST "Thinking Tool" as part of a "Daily Pat on the Back". Essentially, now students must use this tool to plan for upcoming events rather than simply evaluating past events.

Lesson 3-Activity 1: *Setting Personal Goals*

Materials

- BASIC CRITICAL THINKING SKILLS WORKSHEET (ROPES-13). Also referred to as CST "Thinking Tool"
- GOALS WORKSHEET (ROPES-14)
- EVALUATING and SELECTING APPROPRIATE ACTIONS (ROPES-20)
- ACTION PLAN CARD (ROPES-21)

Set Up

The triangle in the CST "Thinking Tool" is the desired outcome (or goal) that the student wants to achieve. The square is the action plan or steps the student must perform in order to obtain the outcome. The circle provides clarification about the timeline and setting conditions for performing the actions to obtain the goal (e.g., the reasons why a certain action plan and outcome is desired).

Step for Participation

1. Model the process of using the CST "Thinking Tool" for *goal setting* by backward chaining a "personal goal".

   a. First, identify a desired goal and write it in the *triangle* on the white board (e.g. goal or outcome, "I want to have a clean desk or lose 5 pounds").

   b. Next, model how to develop the action plan by writing the steps or actions needed to accomplish the goal in the square.

      i. On the board in the blank square, write down 2-4 steps or actions that would be necessary to meet the desired goal or outcome (triangle).

      ii. For example: To lose five pounds, the desired outcome, certain actions are needed such as eliminating high fat foods, replacing them with low fat foods, exercising, drinking more water, etc.

      iii. It should be pointed out that if the actions in the square did not "change" then the outcome/goal in the triangle would not occur.

      iv. Point out that continuing to eat Twinkies and watching TV instead of eliminating Twinkies and exercising will produce different outcomes (triangles).

2. Next model how to identify the context and needed resources in the circle portion of the CST "Thinking Tool" on the board.

   a. This includes the "reasons" (circle) to develop an action plan in the first place.

   b. For example, if the outcome is to lose five pounds then some reasons (circle) could be to feel better, sleep better, reduce cholesterol, look better, live longer etc.

3. Using the directional arrows, show the students the relationship between the reasons (circle), the action plan (square), the goal (triangle) and how this can be used to set personal goals.

   a. Most of the time we set a goal and then work backwards to identify what we need to do to accomplish the goal.

   b. Explain this to students so they can begin to learn how to set their own goals and develop plans to meet those goals.

4. A Group Activity may be done at this time with the GOALS WORKSHEET which is a variation of a Cluster Organizer. The difference being that this graphic organizer is shaped like a Cluster Organizer but uses a *circle* in the center to identify the "Situation" and triangles as the potential goals "Outcomes" positioned around the circle.

   a. On the board, draw a GOALS WORKSHEET with "possible goals" in the triangles that are positioned around the center circle.

   b. Have students generate a list of possible goals (triangles) and record the students' ideas in the outer triangles on the board.

   c. Ask students to think about goals that can be accomplished within a month.

      • Some goals could be related to grades or organizational skills, some related to trying new activities, some related to social skills, e.g., I will bring my grade in science up to a C; I will try out for band; I will meet three new people; I will keep my backpack clean for a month, etc.

      • Goals can also be selected from the EFQ Self Evaluation that was completed in Unit 1.

Figure 3.3 Sample Goals Worksheet

5. Next, using the CST "Thinking Tool" have students identify their own personal goal.

   a. This should be something that will result in a positive outcome they want to accomplish and that is attainable within the coming four weeks or prior to the end of the reporting period.

   b. Have them write this in the triangle of their own CST "Thinking Tool"

   c. Define the word goal as the outcome the students want to obtain or earn.

6. Next, have the students identify the behaviors or actions (square) they must do in order to earn the reward or achieve the goal. Have them record this on their CST "Thinking Tool".

   a. Be specific. For example, if the desired outcome is to be able to bring the math grade up to a B, the actions the student must perform in order to earn that grade is to complete and turn in all homework, study for unit tests, go to afterschool tutoring for concepts that are not understood, etc.

    b. Have the students write these steps or behaviors in the square.

    c. The students may need assistance with breaking down activities or tasks into "action plans."

7. Finally, have the students identify any specifics or reasons regarding who, what, when, and where they would perform the actions. In this example, the circle might indicate:

    a. Who: Me, Mr. Smith (Math Tutor), Mom and Dad (ride home)

    b. What: math book, daily planner, index cards, homework folder, afterschool tutoring program, homework summary sheet.

    c. When: daily when tutoring is offered

    d. Where: home, school, afterschool center

8. After the students complete the CST "Thinking Tool" goal setting activity they should place the form in a sheet protector and put it in their binders for easy access and review.

9. Give the students blank triangles so they can write their goals on them. Then post the goals (triangles) on a "Goals Wall" bulletin board with a goal post. Once the goal is met, the triangle is moved to inside the goal post.

10. Check in on progress weekly or daily if appropriate. Have the students report back to the group on how they are progressing on their goal.

    a. Have the students to use the CST "Thinking Tool" as a reference, as needed, to remind them of the "action to outcome" relationship.

    b. If motivation is low, the reminder can be helpful to increase performance of the actions required.

11. Repeat the use of the CST "Thinking Tool" for short term goals several times and review it each time the students reach a goal and earn the stated rewards or outcome.

    a. As the teacher, it may be necessary to create outcomes or rewards that you can deliver if the students' goals are met.

    b. Be creative and positive and understand this is a skill students are going to have to learn to be successful.

   c. At first they should set goals that they can easily attain so that goal setting and planning become intrinsically rewarding.

   d. Failure to meet set goals leads to discouragement, so we want to avoid this by helping students to set reasonable goals.

12. Consider setting weekly classroom goals such as "all students pass binder checks" or "no student absences for the week."

   a. If something occurs where the students do not meet their classroom goals, review what occurred to prevent attainment of that goal.

   b. For example, if students fail to complete the HOMEWORK SUMMARY SHEET on Thursday, this failure to complete the action can result in a loss of the Reward Points.

13. Once this process of setting and accomplishing short term goals is solid and effective, move into setting goals for other academic outcomes (e.g. completing a book report on time, etc.) and setting longer term goals.

   a. When you move into longer term goals, it is critical to review where the students are on attainment of the goal on a regular basis.

   b. The CST "Thinking Tool" is the students' reminder of the goal and what they need to do to earn or obtain it.

   c. It should be readily accessible and reviewed regularly.

   d. It can be helpful to have the students check off the steps in the square or visually chart their progress toward the goal.

Figure 3.4 Sample CST "Thinking Tool" for Goal Setting

CST "Thinking Tool" for Self-Evaluation and Goal Setting

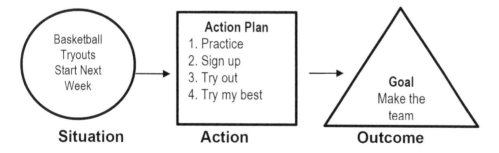

Situation   **Action**   **Outcome**

Lesson 3-Activity 2: *Identifying Areas for Self-Improvement*

Materials

- GOALS WORKSHEET (ROPES 14)
- ACTION PLAN CARD (ROPES 21)
- SELF-IMPROVEMENT CONTRACT (ROPES 24)

Steps for Participation

1. Start by having students complete an ACTION PLAN CARD for each goal identified on their GOALS WORKSHEET.

2. Have the students identify a location(s) to keep the ACTION PLAN CARDS such as a pocket binder so they can be used and referenced often.

3. As the students utilize the strategy outlined on the ACTION PLAN CARD, provide positive feedback and encouragement. Consider providing extra Reward Points.

4. If a student is not using the strategy specified on the ACTION PLAN CARD, first give cues such as tapping or pointing to the card. If nonverbal cues don't work, then review the sequence with the student and determine if the ACTION PLAN needs to be revised.

5. The ACTION PLAN CARD may eventually cue the students to stop and think about what they should do *prior* to engaging in the problematic behavior.

Figure 3.5 Sample ACTION PLAN CARD

ACTION PLAN CARD

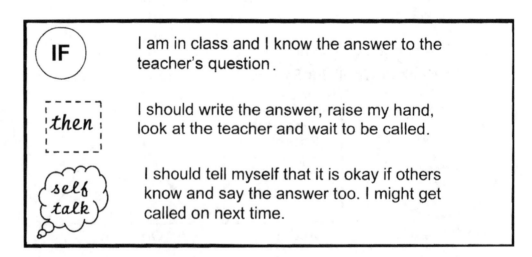

IF	I am in class and I know the answer to the teacher's question.
then	I should write the answer, raise my hand, look at the teacher and wait to be called.
self talk	I should tell myself that it is okay if others know and say the answer too. I might get called on next time.

Lesson 4: Problem Solving

Content Information for Teachers

It may be necessary to place immediate emphasis on problematic behaviors being exhibited by students if they are interfering with learning. As part of a comprehensive behavior intervention plan, the students must learn to look objectively at their own behaviors. This can be done using the CST "Thinking Tool" as structured in the EVALUATING AND RESOLVING PROBLEMATIC BEHAVIOR WORKSHEET. By learning to evaluate their own problematic behaviors, students will begin to see the relationship between behaviors and negative consequences. In this context they will learn to identify their emotions, stress, and sensory needs as well. They will learn to self-manage behaviors and choose more effective actions in the future. They will also gain valuable insight into the affect their behaviors have on others, thus learning the valuable skill of perspective taking.

Materials

- BASIC CRITICAL THINKING SKILLS WORKSHEET (ROPES-13). Also referred to as CST "Thinking Tool"
- GOALS WORKSHEET (ROPES-13).
- EVALUATING AND RESOLVING PROBLEMATIC BEHAVIORS (ROPES 17)
- BEHAVIOR PROBLEM SOLVING WORKSHEET (ROPES 18-19)
- EVALUATING AND SELECTING APPROPRIATE ACTIONS (ROPES 20)
- ACTION PLAN CARD (ROPES 21)
- SELF-IMPROVEMENT CONTRACT (ROPES 24)

Lesson 4 - Activity 1: *Reflecting on Individual Student Behavior*

Set Up

If using this with an individual student, follow the same process as described below, but relate it to their actual behaviors of concern.   Make sure that the implementer is not emotionally charged or upset with the student in any way when the lesson is taking place, it might be best to have a neutral/uninvolved person conduct the lesson in order to avoid issues. Typically, when students engage in "maladaptive behaviors," there are consequences that are implemented in an attempt to decrease or interrupt the behavior. Once consequences have been implemented, as indicated by the individualized behavior intervention plan, and student has been given the opportunity to de-escalate, they could fill out the EVALUATING AND RESOLVING PROBLEMATIC BEHAVIOR WORKSHEET. Often this can become part of the restitution procedure specified in the behavior plan to ensure that students are emotionally ready to resume the school day or activity.

Step for Participation

1. When reflecting on problem behaviors, be sure the alternative pathways that describe the better choice are realistic and practical.

2. At first, completing the components of the EVALUATING AND RESOLVING PROBLEMATIC BEHAVIORS worksheet with the students will require ongoing guidance and feedback.

   a. Remember reflecting on "poor choices" should be a teaching experience not a punitive or negative experience.

   b. Once the students have experience with the process, they should complete the worksheet independently, with feedback after the entire worksheet is completed.

   c. Students may need to practice filling in the worksheet many times before they are able to complete the worksheet independently.

3. Begin by recording the CST "Thinking Tool" sequence that occurred, as objectively as possible.

   a. Next draw a second square to triangle sequence underneath to represent "other" optional choices that could have been made or could be made in the future.

   b. Complete as many square to triangle sequences as can be thought of to show the students that there are always other options or choices that could be made given a single circle (situation).

   c. This could be hard for them to understand because they typically think they made the "right" choice, but continue to encourage them to participate and think about options that could result in better outcomes in the future.

4. Students should practice this process for several different behaviors to promote the generalization of this concept.

   a. The targeted behaviors do not need to be extreme or dangerous. They could be behaviors such as talking out in class, interrupting others, making clicking sounds, etc.

5. NOTE: The future goal is for students to complete the worksheet independently, with 80% accuracy. The student/teacher responses should correspond at least 80% of the time. Eventually the goal is for this process to directly result in the decrease of the targeted maladaptive behaviors.

6. Eventually students may "think" through this process prior to engaging in maladaptive behaviors or to adjust their future behavior.

   a. If students continue to need the worksheet to organize their thoughts, this is acceptable.

7. NOTE: The goal of this activity is to teach students a process for reflecting on their actions and choices. The goal of this activity is not to change behaviors immediately or stop a problem behavior. This is long term process. Patience and encouragement with the students should be the primary focus. There are always consequences for poor choices. Writing them out in the triangles will seem less punitive to the students, thus allowing them to truly reflect on their "choices" rather than being discouraged.

Figure 3.6 Sample SELECTING APPROPRIATE ACTIONS FORM

Evaluating and Selecting Appropriate Actions

Situation:

Math teacher will be gone for a week and a substitute teacher will be here.

Possible Action:

Do not come to school that week. Do home study instead.

Likely Outcome:

Avoid stress, get work done. Not see friends or play chess.

Possible Action:

Stay in resource room for that period.

Likely Outcome:

Avoid stress, get work done. See friends and play chess.

Possible Action:

Go to math and do the best I can.

Likely Outcome:

High level of stress, poor work performance, possible meltdown.

Figure 3.7 Sample SELECTING APPROPRIATE ACTIONS FORM

Evaluating and Resolving Problematic Behavior

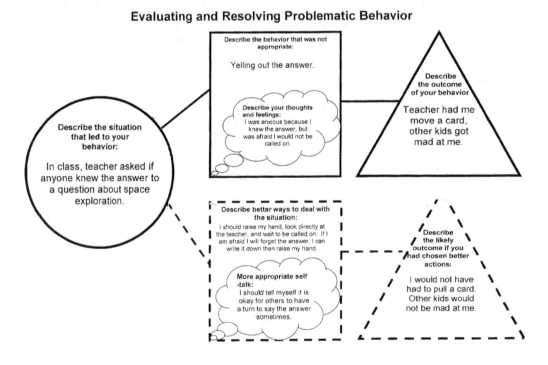

Describe the situation that led to your behavior:

In class, teacher asked if anyone knew the answer to a question about space exploration.

Describe the behavior that was not appropriate:

Yelling out the answer.

Describe your thoughts and feelings:
I was anxious because I knew the answer, but was afraid I would not be called on.

Describe the outcome of your behavior

Teacher had me move a card, other kids got mad at me.

Describe better ways to deal with the situation:
I should raise my hand, look directly at the teacher, and wait to be called on. If I am afraid I will forget the answer, I can write it down then raise my hand.

More appropriate self-talk:
I should tell myself it is okay for others to have a turn to say the answer sometimes.

Describe the likely outcome if you had chosen better actions:

I would not have had to pull a card. Other kids would not be mad at me.

Unit 4: Organizing Information from Lecture and Text Material

Objectives

- Students will learn how to use graphic organizers to help them better recall and organize information so it can be integrated with other knowledge for functional use.

- They will learn to summarize information based on their experiences, what they hear and what they read.

Content Information for Teachers

The ability to summarize and restate information, including verbal instructions, text, and personal experiences, follow multi-step directions, and complete multi-step tasks, without requiring additional prompting from another person is a difficulty that inhibits school success.

Many students struggle with recalling information that was presented orally or through reading text. This deficit limits their ability to be successful and independent with test taking, providing oral reports and written reports, homework and independent projects. Teaching strategies for outlining and summarizing information using graphic organizers have been demonstrated to be effective techniques to promote success in these areas.

Generally, students have more success recalling personal experiences as opposed to information they hear about or read about. Therefore, it is important to teach students to outline and summarize real life experiences first as a foundation for more complex information found in core subject areas such as social studies, language arts and science.

Often, it is easier for students to summarize information they are hearing as opposed to information they are reading. Therefore, the lessons will begin by teaching students to outline and summarize information through verbal input (lecture) before working on summarizing information presented in written text. In addition, developmentally the ability to provide a verbal summary precedes the ability to provide a written summary so this skill should be worked on first.

Unit 4: Lesson 1 | <u>Lesson 1</u>: **Using Graphic Organizers to Summarize and Recall Personal Experiences and Events**

Materials

- T CHARTS

Lesson 1-Activity 1: *Definition of a Summary*

Steps for Participation

1. Ask students to define the word "summary" or "summarize."
   a. Write down the definition on the board.
   b. According to Websters, a summary is the restating of the main ideas or points in as few words as possible.
2. Discuss why it is a useful or a good skill to have to be able to summarize.
   a. Helps you get to the point.
   b. Helps to share information or an experience with someone else in as few words as possible.
   c. Helps you study or take notes.
   d. Helps you to make an outline for writing so you can organize your ideas.
   e. Helps you organize ideas for an oral report.
   f. Helps you understand the main points of a story or lesson.
   g. Helps you understand the "big picture".
   h. Helps you recall important information for a test.

Lesson 1-Activity 2: *Using T CHARTS to Summarize Tasks and Instructions*

Steps for Participation

1. Explain to students they will be learning how to use a T CHART to summarize and recall events, information and instructions.
2. Draw a T CHART on the board.
   a. Topic/Title: "What I Did."
   b. Left Side: Main Idea(s)
   c. Right Side: Details or Keywords

3. Give students a simple instruction or task to complete. For example, tell students to take off one shoe and put it on the desk. Then ask them what they did.

   a. On the left side of the T CHART write "took off shoe"

   b. On the right side of the T CHART write the details. Sample responses could be: untied laces, pulled off, put on desk (three details).

4. Repeat this with several other simple instructions, such as, "Get ready for math," "Find something interesting in your backpack," "Draw a happy face," "Sharpen your pencil," "Wash your hands," etc.

5. Help students to attend to the details and specific actions that were taken to get to the final step.

   a. Students may tend to describe the final outcome (took off shoe or put candy bar on desk) rather than be able to describe the individual steps they took to complete the task.

6. Next, ask students to refer back to the completed T CHARTS in preparation for an oral summary.

   a. Call on individual students to share what they did with the group.

   b. Every student should be able to answer the questions accurately by referring to the T CHART.

7. Explain to students that they used the T CHART to organize information and details related to following instructions and completing tasks, but later the same strategy will be used for complex assignments, projects, note taking and studying in school. In later Units this strategy will also be used to help with recalling conversations, instructions and assist in social situations.

Lesson 1-Activity 3: *Using a T Chart to Recall Previous Experiences*

Set up

The Teacher will use a T CHART to summarize a personal experience.

Steps for Participation

1. Draw a T CHART on the board and label it, "What I Did Today."

2. On the left side write three main chunks of the day

   a. before work

   b. morning at work

   c. afternoon at work

3. On the right side bullet point "keywords" that provide the details about what occurred within each of those time frames. Samples include:

   a. Before work: I brushed my teeth, made my lunch, said good bye to family and drove to school.

   b. Morning at work: checked email, called two parents, made photocopies

   c. Afternoon at work: graded papers, gave a test, called dentist

4. After the T CHART is completed, then model a short oral summary of "What I did Today" by referencing the keywords from the T CHART.

5. The oral summary should be a brief summary of each of the main points. This exercise is to summarize the main points using the keywords, not to describe in detail each component.

6. Examples and Non-examples: Next give an example of a correct summary and how to find keywords and then give an example of an incorrect summary.

   a. The incorrect summary example could exclude or skip main points or spend too much time on an unimportant detail or summarize the information in a random or disorganized manner.

   b. As this is explained to the students be sure to illustrate the example and non-example as clearly as possible.

   c. Later the students will be asked to give a correct summary example and also an incorrect summary example.

7. Give students a T CHART to complete. Explain that the organizer will be used to help them to recall and summarize information and experiences from their day.

   a. Have students label the T CHART "What I did today."

   b. On the Left side have them write "Before school I___", then "When I got to School I___" and last "At lunch I___"

8. Start this as a group and ask students to write three details or "keywords" about each chunk of their day.

  a. Students should then share their keywords from their T CHART with the group, even if they are all similar.

  b. Attempt to use peers to provide model examples for the students who need additional practice.

9. Then ask several students to use their T CHART to provide an oral summary of the events of their day to the group.

10. Have the students save the completed T CHARTS for the next activity.

Lesson 1-Activity 4: *Using a T CHART to Write a Summary about a Personal Experience*

Steps for Participation

1. For this activity, use the T CHARTS from the previous activity, or generate new ones about something recent and relevant to your class (e.g. an assembly or field trip that was taken).

2. Start by modeling for the students how to use a T CHART to support a written summary.

  a. The teacher should write a summary paragraph on the board using the "keywords" in the T CHART as the guide for sentence content. The teacher can model an example of a good summary and a poor, disorganized, over detailed summary to show an example and non-example to the students.

  b. Read the two examples to the class and have them vote on which summary would get an "A," and have them explain why.

3. Then, have the students write a 5-7 sentence paragraph summarizing the experience they wrote about in Lesson 1-Activity 3 using the keywords from their T CHART.

4. Select key students to read their summaries to the group and discuss whether their summaries had all the critical information based on their keywords and have them pinpoint any missing information.

5. Explain to the students that a good summary gives an overview of an experience or topic with a few key details to give the listener or reader a "picture" or understanding of the experience.

6. Refer back to the teacher's example of a poor summary and explain why it was not a good summary.

Lesson 1-Activity 5: *Using a T CHART to Summarize a Personal Experience*

Steps for Participation

1. Select a topic as a group to summarize such as My Favorite Vacation or The Scariest Moment of My Life, etc.

2. Use a teacher example or have a student volunteer complete the process with the group before having students complete it independently: See example:

   a. TITLE: My Favorite Vacation: Going to Hawaii.

   b. Left Side (Main Ideas): Hotel, Food, Beach.

   c. Right Side (Details/Keywords):

      i. Hotel: beautiful, great service, great view,

      ii. Food: unique, delicious, fast service,

      iii. Beach: not crowded, relaxing, waves.

3. Next have students complete their own T CHART with the selected topic using the same process as above.

Figure 4.1 T CHART Summarizing a Personal Experience

My Favorite Vacation: Gong to Hawaii

Main Ideas	Details
Hotel	Beautiful, Great Service and View
Food	Unique, Delicious, Fast Service
Beach	Not Crowded, Relaxing, Waves

Lesson 1-Activity 6: *Using a T CHART to Give an Oral Summary of a Personal Experience*

Steps for Participation

1. Students will use their T CHART created in Activity 5 to provide a short oral summary to the group.

   a. Summaries should take 1-2 minutes at the most.

   b. Use a timer to keep track of how long the summaries take each student to present.

2. As each student uses the T CHART to orally give the summary to the group, the teacher or a student volunteer will complete a T CHART on the board writing down the Main Ideas on the left side and corresponding Details or Keywords on the right side.

    a. OPTIONAL: Each student could complete a T CHART as the summary is presented. This is giving them practice "Taking Summary Notes", which is a skill that will be taught in future lessons.

3. After each student reads the summary compare the two T CHARTS to see if the student's T CHART matches the group's T CHART that was created on the board.

    a. Help students to see that there should be similarities.

4. Repeat this with 4-6 different student summaries.

Lesson 1-Activity 7: *Using a T CHART to Write a Summary about a Personal Experience*

Steps for Participation

1. In previous activities students have created a T CHART on a chosen topic outlining main ideas and keywords related to details. Using those T CHARTS, they have given an oral summary to the group. Now, they will generate a written summary.

2. Using the same topic and T CHART, have students write a short 5-7 sentence paragraph summarizing their personal experience.

3. Have students read their summaries.

    a. As each student reads the summary, recreate a T CHART as in the above activity and compare the student's and the group's T CHARTS.

4. The reason to compare the two T CHARTS is to illustrate that the content of the written and oral summaries should be organized and give an accurate portrayal of key information to the listener or reader.

5. This is also an exercise to teach students how to organize information for note taking.

| Unit 4: Lesson 2 | Lesson 2: Creating Written Summaries from Lectures and Taking Notes |

Content Information

Many students are able to listen to the lectures and discussions, but are unable to extract any meaningful information from them. Some students may be able to fill out the organizer while listening to the lecture or while reading a text. However, this shifting of attention from listening or reading to writing can be very difficult for some students. Some students may be more successful by listening to a segment of the lecture, while others may prefer to read a section of the text and then immediately fill in the organizer by recalling important information from that section. Breaking the text or lecture up into smaller segments will help while students learn this process.

Lesson 2-Activity 1: *Using T CHARTS to Summarize Information from Lectures*

Materials

- 6-8 selected paragraphs on various topics, preferably from student textbooks or current events
- White boards
- T CHARTS

Set up

Individual white boards may be used for this activity so that students can easily and quickly share responses with the teacher for immediate feedback in a group setting. Be prepared to read paragraphs from a common text in core subject areas such as English, Science, or Social Studies texts. Students will use T CHARTS to summarize information from the lecture. Complete this process with 4-6 lecture topics before moving on. The desired outcome of this process is to give students strategies to provide oral or written summaries of important information.

Steps for Participation

1. Give students a T CHART or use individual white boards and draw a T CHART on the board.
2. Have students label the T CHART with the title and the left column labeled "Main Ideas" and the right column labeled "Details."
3. A student volunteer could read the passage as the other students and the teacher complete their T CHARTS.
4. The T CHART should be titled with the main topic of the passage, such as Mammals or Ancient Egypt.

5. As the passage is read have the students complete the T CHART.

   a. On the left side of the T CHART write Main Idea(s) and ask students to describe what the paragraph was about in 3-5 word phrases and write their responses on the board.

   b. On the right side of the T CHART write Details and ask students to describe 2-3 details per main topic and write their responses on the board.

6. Read one paragraph from the selected text at a time and stop to allow time for students to take notes using the T CHART.

7. Once the passage is read, review the students' T CHARTS and compare them for accuracy.

8. Repeat this process until students can easily give summary phrases or Main Ideas (Left Side) and at least five key Details (Right Side) from each paragraph read to them.

Lesson 2-Activity 2: *Using T CHARTS to Create Oral Summaries from Lectures*

Steps for Participation

1. Using the T CHARTS that students created from the above activity, have them give short oral summaries to the group.

   a. Each summary should include 2-3 Main Ideas (left side) and 2-3 details for each Details (right side).

2. Recreate a T CHART on the board to illustrate the points the students cover in their oral summaries while they are presenting the information.

3. Compare the students' T CHARTS and the ones they created by the group and discuss them.

4. Repeat this process with 4-6 lecture topics.

Lesson 2-Activity 3: *Using T CHARTS to Create Written Summaries from Lectures*

Steps for Participation

1. After students have shared their summaries orally, have them each write a 5-7 sentence summary paragraph using the information outlined in the T CHARTS.

2. Have one or two students read their written summaries on the passage and create a T CHART on the board as they read.

3. Compare and discuss the T CHARTS and explain that there should be continuity and similarities in the T CHARTS.

Lesson 2-Activity 4: *Using T CHARTS to, Summarize Information from Written Text*

Materials

- T CHARTS
- Photo copies of text passages

Set up

Students should have individual white boards. Be prepared to have photocopied written materials from relevant texts (social studies, science, literature, current events, etc.) to distribute to each student. It may be necessary to use nonacademic topics or preferred topics at first before using academic subjects. Students will use T CHARTS to summarize information from the written materials and text. Complete this process with 6-8 written text topics before moving on. The desired outcome of this process is to give students strategies to provide oral or written summaries of important information.

Steps for Participation

1. Give students a T CHART to take personal notes and draw a T CHART on the board.
   a. The T CHART should be titled with the Topic, such as Mammals or Ancient Egypt and each column should be labeled
   b. Have students label the left column "Main Ideas" and the right column "Details"

2. Have students read one paragraph at a time to themselves and stop.

3. Have students complete the T CHARTS based on what they read.

4. Students can complete the T CHARTS as a large group, in small groups, or individually if preferred.

5. Once the students have read the passage and completed the T CHARTS ask for volunteers to share their responses.

6. Discuss similarities between students T CHARTS and discuss accuracy of the summaries.

a. Be sure to check in with all students on this if doing this lesson in a group.

7. Complete this process until students can easily give 3-4 summary phrases or "Main Ideas" (Left Side) and at least 5 key "Details" (Right Side) from the text.

Lesson 2-Activity 5: *Using T CHARTS to Create Oral Summaries from Text*

Steps for Participation

1. Using the T CHARTS that students created in Activity 4, have selected students provide short oral summaries to the group. It is suggested that students be given a variety of passages to summarize.

   a. Each oral summary should include 2-3 Main Ideas (Left Side) and 1-2 Details (Right Side) for each main idea.

2. As students give their oral summaries have the other students create their own T CHARTS as they are following along with the oral presentation.

3. Following the oral presentations discuss the similarities and differences between the students' T CHARTS who listened to the presentation to determine if they focused on similar points.

Lesson 2-Activity 6: *Using T CHARTS to Write Summaries from Text*

Steps for Participation

1. After students have shared their summaries orally by using the T CHART, then have them write a 5-7 sentence summary paragraph.

2. Create a written template for students to follow when constructing a written summary with correct transition phrases and structural supports.

3. Have select students read their summaries and create a T CHART on the board as they read. Individual students can create T CHARTS as well.

4. Discuss the T CHARTS and explain that there should be continuity and similarities in the T CHARTS created by the group and the T CHART created by the student.

5. Repeat this process with 6-8 types of written materials that are relevant to their age and classes.

Notes:_____

UNIT 5: Time Management and Prioritization

Objectives

- Students will learn to estimate the amount of time activities will take to complete.
- Students will learn to prioritize activities.
- Students will learn to set short and long term goals.

Content Information for Teachers

Time Management is a critical skill in effective planning. To schedule any activity, one must first determine or estimate the amount of time it will take to complete it.

Successful instruction in these areas requires committed teachers and parents who will be consistent with coaching and support while students learn the R.O.P.E.S. of Time Management and Prioritization.

Materials

- TIME JOURNAL (ROPES-10).
- VENN DIAGRAM (ROPES-11).
- BASIC CRITICAL THINKING SKILLS WORKSHEET (ROPES-13). Also referred to as CST "Thinking Tool"
- GOALS WORKSHEET (ROPES-14).
- DECISION MATRIX FOR PRIORITIZATION (ROPES-13).
- PRIORITIES LADDER (ROPES-13).
- TIME MANAGEMENT SYSTEMS: MONTHLY PLANNING CALENDARS (ROPES-18), DAILY SCHEDULES (ROPES-09).

Lesson 1: Time Estimation and "Guess-timation"

Set Up

Students will learn to use a TIME JOURNAL. Explain to students that the TIME JOURNAL serves four functions.

1. It will establish how long certain basic tasks and activities will take to complete. Once a comprehensive log is established, the students can use it to estimate the amount of time to allocate for specific tasks. This preparation will then allow the students to independently put tasks into the daily schedule or calendar.

2. It will provide a list of activities to refer to when students are learning how to "guesstimate" the amount of time required for novel tasks and activities, as discussed below.

3. It will provide practice and an opportunity to see how well students do at estimation. The students will be able to compare how long they thought a task would take to how long it actually took. Over time and with practice, they should become increasingly better at time estimation.

4. It will be a valuable tool in helping to improve efficiency. When tasks take longer than expected students will learn to evaluate the reasons by identifying the competing behaviors and environmental distractions which will help them to develop plans for improving efficiency at these tasks in the future.

5. NOTE: This lesson will take several days to complete and will require students to do some "homework" as they estimate and record the completion time for various activities across their day.

Unit 5: Lesson 1 — Lesson 1-Activity 1: *Time Estimation*

Materials

- TIME JOURNAL (ROPES-10)
- Timers

Steps for Participation

1. Give students TIME JOURNALS and create one on the board.

2. Begin by explaining to the students what time estimation is and the purpose(s) of the TIME JOURNAL that was stated above

   a. This will help students learn how to make accurate time estimations which is critical to helping them plan and organize projects and tasks.

3. Brainstorm with the students several important reasons good time management is important to school and work success.

4. Examples could be

   a. Be on time so you don't get fired

   b. Avoid unexcused tardies

   c. Complete assignments and tasks that teachers and bosses require

   d. Schedule and make short and long terms goals and plans

e. Use time wisely so there is time to have fun after work is completed

f. Helps to get and maintain good grades

5. On the board in the TIME JOURNAL generate a list of 5-10 simple activities/tasks that could be done in class.

a. For example, putting on socks and shoes, writing the pledge of allegiance, sharpening a pencil, reading a paragraph in a book.

6. Have the students "estimate" the amount of time each of these activities will take them.

a. Have students write their estimation on their TIME JOURNAL.

b. The teacher can record the estimation on the board.

7. Next, have the students and teacher complete the tasks listed on the board, recording the start time and end time of each

a. NOTE: This can be done where the whole class performs each task using a timer or stopwatch to record their own personal times, or it can be done by having one student complete the task while being timed.

8. The students will record the start time, end time, and total time that the task took on the TIME JOURNAL and compare their estimates to the actual time.

9. The teacher should then lead a discussion about estimation, including why certain tasks took longer than they estimated or less time than they estimated.

a. The teacher should also explain and discuss how making "good guesses" or estimates helps in planning and organizing the day.

10. Discuss with the students *reasons* their estimations might have been over or under (e.g., distractions, lack of focus, not prepared, missing materials etc.)

11. Homework:

a. Have students generate a list of 4-5 tasks and routines that they complete on a daily basis at home.

b. These should be tasks or routines that are familiar to the students (do not use novel or irregular routines at this point).

c. Some examples of tasks include: taking a shower, making a sandwich or bowl of cereal, driving/riding to school, brushing teeth, getting dressed, putting on shoes, cleaning their room, etc.

12. While in class, ask students to estimate how long each of these tasks/routines will take them to complete.

    a. For homework they will need to record start times, end times and total time for each task/routine. Have them record the estimations on the form.

13. In Class Follow-Up:

    a. Lead students in a discussion about their estimations.

    b. Discuss those estimations that were significantly over or under the original guesses.

    c. Have students share why they think their time was less or more than they originally estimated.

    d. Discuss and define "procrastination" and how distractions may have impacted the overall time that tasks took to complete and ways of improving efficiency as an introduction to concepts that will follow.

        i. Have students identify if they have developed procrastination habits. Help them to identify this obstacle and ways to avoid it in the future.

        ii. Have students brainstorm reasons and ways they procrastinate as a way to help them become aware of habits they may need to change.

        iii. Discuss strategies that can be used when feelings of avoidance occur such as setting up a "self-reward" after task completion, etc.

14. For gross overestimations (i.e., students estimated that it would take far longer than it actually did), point out that they were more "efficient" than they thought they would be at that task.

    a. Ask if there was anything that contributed to their efficiency. Did they like the task or was it easy? Did they do anything that allowed them to complete the task more quickly, such as eliminating distractions?

    b. This will introduce the concept of "efficiency" which will be elaborated on later.

15. For gross underestimations (i.e., students estimated that it would take far less time than it did), point out that they were not as efficient at that task as they predicted.

    a. Ask what obstacles occurred that might have decreased efficiency such as distractions, not motivated to do the task, etc.

    b. Brainstorm with students additional strategies that may help with improving efficiency.

Lesson 1-Activity 2: *Guesstimation*

Materials

- VENN DIAGRAM (ROPES-11)
- TIME JOURNAL (ROPES-10)
- T CHART

Steps for Participation

1. Ask students to share their methods for determining how long an unknown task might take them to complete.

   a. For example, when a teacher assigns a project unlike anything they have done before, how do they "guess" how long it will take them?

2. Guide the students to talk about how they use their knowledge about similar activities or how they may ask someone who has performed the task previously.

3. Present the VENN DIAGRAM and show the students how to use it to compare and contrast a novel activity with a known previous activity.

4. Fill in the name of a novel task on the *right side* of the VENN DIAGRAM.

   a. For example, making scrambled eggs could be the novel activity.

   b. Have the students go to their TIME JOURNALS and pick an activity that they think is most similar to the new activity.

   c. Once they have selected a similar activity such as making a sandwich, write it on the left side of the VENN DIAGRAM titled "previous experience" circle of the VENN DIAGRAM.

   d. Have the students describe the two tasks, writing the similarities in the overlapping section and the differences in the left side of the VENN DIAGRAM.

   e. Make sure to include how much time the known previous activity took to complete.

   f. Based on the comparison, the students should be able to "guesstimate" how much time the novel task should take.

5. If the students have a hard time choosing one appropriate similar activity from the samples on the TIME JOURNAL, provide assistance by narrowing it down to two possible activities from the TIME JOURNAL that are similar to the novel task.

6. Using the VENN DIAGRAM, they will learn to identify the most similar task from the TIME JOURNAL independently.

7. The students can fine tune "guesstimation" skills the same way they did with estimation.

   a. This involves tracking guesstimates on the TIME JOURNAL and comparing them to the actual time.

   b. For a long task, a reasonable goal for this skill should be for guesstimating within 5-10 minutes of the actual time required about 70% of the time. Shorter tasks will require proportional guesstimation.

Lesson 1-Activity 3: *Determining "Work Time" for Homework*

NOTE: This activity will take several days to complete as it will require students to self-monitor their homework completion and report back information over several days or weeks.

Steps for Participation

1. The students will complete the procedure for estimating, or guesstimating how much "work time" each of the specific homework assignments will require.

   a. This could be done as a group with some general assignments that the teacher creates or with actual assignments given by their teachers in other classes.

2. OPTIONAL: One assignment could be for students to bring their TIME JOURNALS filled in with assignments they were given from their other classes to their study skills class and complete this assignment in class.

3. For complex assignments such as term papers and book reports, the students may need assistance in chunking them into steps and estimating the amount of work time will be required to complete each chunk of the assignment.

   a. The strategies for teaching students to chunk are covered in Unit 6 – Project Management.

4. The estimated or guesstimated "work time" for each assignment should be written on the TIME JOURNAL.

5. The students should complete the assignments and fill in the "actual time" it took them to complete each assignment.

6. Each day, have the students evaluate their estimates/ guesstimates and discuss why an assignment took them longer or shorter than they estimated.

7. On chart paper, make a T CHART of points that students discuss that increased efficiency and that decreased efficiency for homework completion.

8. As items arise, that decreased efficiency, ask students to troubleshoot ways of addressing these issues.

9. On a separate sheet of chart paper, write ideas for improving efficiency and have students keep them in their work folders for reference.

10. Post a list of reminders on the board for student reference.

Lesson 2: Prioritization of Activities and Tasks

Content Information for Teacher

In Unit 3, details about how to teach evaluation skills were presented as the students learned to use the CST "Thinking Tool" to self-evaluate their successes (i.e., Daily Pat on the Back) and to set short term goals. This section further focuses on goal setting and prioritization skills through the use of graphic organizers and a decision matrix. Learning these processes will increase the students' ability to see the relationship between actions and outcomes and compare various tasks and demands in order to determine which activities should be given the most immediate attention. Being able to compare and evaluate various activities and demands is an essential skill for success as a student and in many aspect of adult life.

Prioritization skills are the ability to rank tasks and sequence tasks by "importance" based on the potential positive "bonus" or negative "penalty" outcomes that will result from the completion or non-completion of the task by the deadline. Typically, people prioritize items based on their potential outcomes, penalty or bonus, as well as the urgency, such as how close or far the deadline is. Once the "importance" has been determined, a "value" should be assigned to the items. Using the value, a comparison can be made to other demands so that an order of importance can be determined. The DECISION MATRIX FOR PRIORITIZATION is a visual representation of how to evaluate priorities. It will assist the students with assigning some value to the items they must complete on a daily, weekly, monthly and yearly basis.

Materials

- DECISION MATRIX FOR PRIORITIZATION (ROPES-13).
- BASIC CRITICAL THINKING SKILLS WORKSHEET (ROPES-13). Also referred to as CST "Thinking Tool"
- PRIORITIES LADDER (ROPES-16)

Lesson 2-Activity 1: *Determining Priorities*

Steps for Participation

1. Be prepared to have 4-6 activities or tasks on a to-do list to use to illustrate how to determine priorities. Write the activities on the board.

    a. Some examples include, packing lunch, correcting assignments, putting gas in car, picking up students from school, cleaning the house, attending a meeting, going to dentist, paying bills, buying a gift, grocery shopping, washing the car, etc.

2. Complete the CST "Thinking Tool" on the board for each of the activities.

3. In each circle list the due date or timeframe for each activity or task.

4. Then list each activity or task in a separate square and evaluate the outcome of completing or not completing each square and record it in the triangle.

5. Each triangle should be labeled *high, moderate or low priority*.

6. Explain to students what each box means on the DECISION MATRIX FOR PRIORITIZATION.

    a. High Bonus or High Penalty with an Immediate Deadline equals a *High Priority*

    b. High Bonus or High Penalty with Distant Deadline equals a *Moderate Priority*

    c. Low Bonus or Low Penalty with an Immediate Deadline equals a *Moderate Priority*

    d. Low Bonus or Low Penalty with Distant Deadline equals a *Low Priority*

7. Identify the potential bonus or penalty for completing or not completing each task and list this in the triangle as well.

8. Discuss with students how the outcome (triangle) helps to determine the level of priority which helps to determine how we make decisions about how to organize our time.

9. Explain to students that some tasks might be more fun but less important than other tasks that might be less fun but more important.

    a. Give several examples and ask students to share their ideas.

10. Then indicate the *potential outcome* of doing vs. not doing the assignment or task in the triangle associated with each square.

    a. This will show students how to determine the potential bonus or penalties associated with each task.

b. Discuss how decisions are made in real life and try to make this a meaningful experience by using real life examples that students can understand.

Lesson 2-Activity 2: *Using the Decision Matrix for Prioritization*

Set up

The activity will require several completed CST "Thinking Tool" samples.

Steps for Participation

1. Create a DECISION MATRIX FOR PRIORITIZATION on the board and give this handout to each student.

2. Refer to the completed CST "Thinking Tool" worksheets or the samples created in the previous activity and then complete the DECISION MATRIX FOR PRIORITIZATION as a group.

3. After each triangle is labeled with the penalty or bonus, then transfer the tasks to the DECISION MATRIX FOR PRIORITIZA-TION in the corresponding box. There should be items and/or activities in each of the four boxes. The matrix will be used to create a priorities ladder in an upcoming activity.

4. Next have students create their own CST "Thinking Tool" to evaluate the importance of actual class assignments homework, projects and various activities they do on a daily basis (e.g., sports practice, club meetings, watch favorite TV shows, play X Box Live Halo with friends etc.

5. Start by having students indicate the assignment or task and the timeframe or due date of it in the circle.

6. Next, have them indicate "complete the assignment or task" in one of the squares and "do not complete the assignment or task" in a square directly below the other square.

7. Then have students indicate the potential outcome of doing vs. not doing the assignment or task in the triangle associated with each square. This will help them to determine the potential bonus or penalties associated with each task.

8. Then create a DECISION MATRIX FOR PRIORITIZATION on the board and ask for a volunteer and repeat process from Lesson 2-Activity 1 with the assignments and tasks they used when they completed the CST "Thinking Tool" in the above steps.

9. Depending on the group, the teacher may want to have the group complete the process on assignments first and then complete the process with other activities.

10. After they complete their individual CST "Thinking Tool" activities have them individually complete the DECISION MATRIX FOR PRIORITIZATION. At this point there should be several items in each of the four boxes.

a. Discuss the items they have put in each box.

11. The DECISION MATRIX FOR PRIORITIZATION should be utilized frequently as part of the daily planning process.

Lesson 2-Activity 3: *Using a Priorities Ladder for Decision Making*
Set Up

Teachers could do a large group activity with the students prior to having the students complete the activity in a small group or individually. This will depend on how quickly the students have learned the previous materials.

Steps for Participation

1. Create a completed DECISION MATRIX FOR PRIORITIZATION on the board with samples in each box or use the one from the previous activity.

2. Have students look at all of the items in the high priority box on the DECISION MATRIX FOR PRIORITIZATION.

    a. Since all of these have high bonus or penalty outcomes, have the students rank them initially by due date, with the items having the most immediate due dates going on the top rung of the PRIORITIES LADDER.

3. Have students go through and rank the moderate priority items and then the low priority items, also placing them on the PRIORITIES LADDER.

4. The students should then have a hierarchy of goals and priorities to work from when updating their daily "to do" lists and monthly calendars.

5. Help the students create reminders and plot tasks and assignments on their calendars.

6. When new tasks or demands are added, they should be evaluated using the criteria from the DECISION MATRIX FOR PRIORITIZATION and placed in the appropriate location on the PRIORITIES LADDER.

    a. This should be discussed each day during the designated planning routine(s).

    b. The class may also have a priorities list posted on the board to reference daily.

7. When the items are completed, they should be removed from the ladder. The remaining items should be moved up a rung.

8. As items are removed, it is an opportunity to re-access prioritization of remaining items and/or add new items.

9. As a class it is important to maintain a PRIORITIES LADDER that is continually updated. This will help students to see the usefulness of keeping track of deadlines and priorities.

10. The teacher may want to have the group complete the process on school assignments first and then complete the process with other items such as extracurricular, etc.

Decision Matrix for Prioritization

	Heavy Bonus or Penalty Outcome	No or Light Bonus or Penalty Outcome
Urgent Deadline	**HIGH PRIORITY** • **BOOK REPORT (100 POINTS)** • **STUDY FOR CALCULUS TEST (50 POINTS)**	**Moderate Priority** • **Spelling test (10 points)** • **Math homework (10 points)** • **Soccer practice and games**
No Deadline or Distant Deadline	**Moderate Priority** • **History term paper (250 points)**	Low Priority • Play Playstation / beat brothers score • Chat with friends online • Extra soccer practice

Figure 5.1. Example of a completed Decision Matrix for Prioritization. All items from the Goals Worksheet are evaluated and placed in the appropriate box on the Decision Matrix so that the student can begin to prioritize the goals.

Priorities Ladder

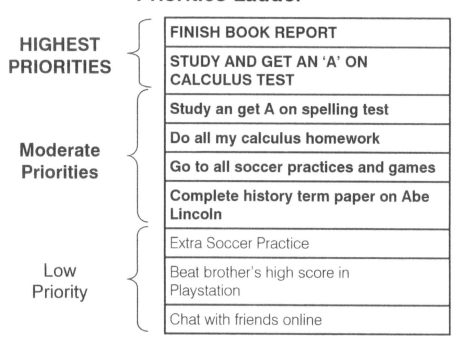

HIGHEST PRIORITIES
- FINISH BOOK REPORT
- STUDY AND GET AN 'A' ON CALCULUS TEST

Moderate Priorities
- Study an get A on spelling test
- Do all my calculus homework
- Go to all soccer practices and games
- Complete history term paper on Abe Lincoln

Low Priority
- Extra Soccer Practice
- Beat brother's high score in Playstation
- Chat with friends online

Figure 5.2 Example of the PRIORITIES LADDER Worksheet. The items from the DECISION MATRIX FOR PRIORITIZATION were ranked here within each priority level.

Lesson 3: *Using a Calendar to Plot Goals*

Content for Teachers

Goals are desired outcomes, including avoidance of problems. Once we identify our goals, we break the steps down and prioritize the things we need to do to accomplish those goals. Because students often have a difficult time predicting outcomes and often do not even think about the potential outcomes of their behavior, they often base their choices on immediate gratification instead of choosing behaviors based on long-term outcomes or goals. Because of deficits in planning and organization, students often fail to engage in goal directed behavior, even when they can identify a desired outcome. Short term goal setting was covered in Unit 3, but now that students have been introduced to time management and prioritization, they can begin the process of long term goal setting.

Lesson 3-Activity 1: *Creating a Monthly Planning Calendar*

Materials

- MONTHLY PLANNING CALENDAR (ROPES 08)

Set Up

It may be beneficial to use a personal schedule or create a mock daily schedule and go through this process as a group prior to having students work in small groups or individually. Typically this will be done during the last class period of the month using the calendar of events for the next month.

Steps for Participation

1. Using the MONTHLY PLANNING CALENDAR have the students write in all regularly occurring events, activities or routines.
   a. If the students are having difficulty use an indirect verbal prompt such as, "Where could you find the information you need?"
2. Next have the students write in any irregular events, activities or routines.
   a. These items may be found in the students' homework management system.
   b. Again, if the students are having difficulty use an indirect verbal prompt such as, "Where could you find the information you need?"
3. If there is a scheduling conflict prompt the student to make adjustments.
   a. Suggest options including using the DECISION MATRIX FOR PRIORITIZATION and the PRIORITIES LADDER.

SEPTEMBER 2004						
Sunday	Monday	Tuesday	Wednesday	Thursday	Friday	Saturday
		1 Research Lincoln 3:00 - 5:00	**2** Research Lincoln 3:00 - 4:00 Soccer Practice 5:00 - 6:00	**3** Study Spelling	**4** Spelling test Free time 4:00 - 6:00	**5** Soccer Game 12:00 - 1:00
6 Research Lincoln 3:00 - 5:00	**7** Write outline for Lincoln Report 4:00 - 6:00	**8** Outline for Lincoln Due	**9** Study Calculus Soccer Practice 5:00 - 6:00	**10** Study Spelling Study Calculus	**11** Spelling Test Free time 4:00 - 6:00	**12** Soccer Game 8:00 - 9:00 Beach Trip 11:00
13 Beach Trip Study Calculus	**14** Calculus test Work on Lincoln rough draft 5:00 - 6:00	**15** Work on Lincoln rough draft 4:00 - 6:00	**16** Study Spelling Soccer Practice 5:00 - 6:00	**17** Rough draft for Lincoln Report Due Study Spelling	**18** **Spelling Test** **Free time** **4:00 - 6:00**	**19** **Soccer Game** **9:00 - 10:00** **Soccer Picnic** **1:00 - 4:00**
20 **Work on Book Report** **9:00 - 12:00** **Movies** **2:00 - 5:00**	**21** **Work on Book Report** **4:00 - 6:00**	**22** **Science Project Due** **Work on Book Report 4:00 - 6:00**	**23** Study Spelling Soccer Practice 5:00 - 6:00	**24** Book Report Due Study Spelling	**25** Spelling Test Free time 4:00 - 6:00	**26** Soccer Game 10:00 - 11:00
27 Revisions to Lincoln Report 9:00-12:00	**28** Prepare final Lincoln Report 5:30 - 6:00 Dr. Apt 3:30	**29** Final Draft for Lincoln Report Due	**30** Study Spelling Soccer Practice 5:00 - 6:00			

Step 1 (Figure 5.3.): The student should begin by looking at the current calendar which already includes all scheduled events (high and low priority). The dark shaded section depicts the area of the calendar that needs to be revised to accommodate the new science assignment. The student should write in the new assignment's due date (indicated here by underlined text).

	Heavy Bonus or Penalty Outcome	No or Light Bonus or Penalty Outcome
Urgent Deadline	**HIGH PRIORITY** • **SCIENCE PROJECT (50 PT)** • **BOOK REPORT (100 PT)**	**Moderate Priority** • **Soccer Game**
No Deadline or Distant Deadline	**Moderate Priority**	Low Priority • Soccer picnic • Movies • Free time

Step 2 (Figure 5.4): Next, the student should complete a revised Decision Matrix for Prioritization. This includes the science project and all other scheduled activities between it's assignment date and due date, those in the darker shaded area of Figure 5.3.

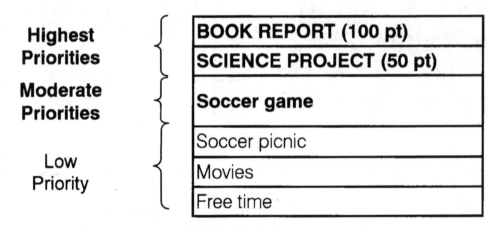

Highest Priorities
Moderate Priorities
Low Priority

BOOK REPORT (100 pt)
SCIENCE PROJECT (50 pt)
Soccer game
Soccer picnic
Movies
Free time

Step 3 (Figure 5.5): The student then completes a revised Priorities Ladder with all of the items from the Decision Matrix. He ranks the book report higher than the science project because it is worth more points.

Lesson 3-Activity 2: *Creating a Daily Schedule Based on Monthly Planning Calendar*

Steps for Participation

1. Each day, the students should look at the MONTHLY PLANNING CALENDAR and create the daily schedule(s) based on the items plotted out on the calendar for that day.

    a. NOTE: A plan may need to be developed to help students track assignments and tasks that are assigned throughout the school day by the various teachers.

2. If there were items on the calendar from the previous day that were not completed or if new items or demands have been added, the students will need to re-prioritize and adjust the monthly calendar accordingly prior to making that day's schedule using the same process described above.

3. Once the items and activities have been ranked, the students can evaluate that day's schedule and determine which item(s), if any, need to be "bumped" and rescheduled on another day in the month.

    a. They should revise the rest of the monthly calendar accordingly (i.e., evaluating and plugging in any bumped items into other days in that month).

4. The students should fill out a DAILY SCHEDULE/CHECK LIST, as described in the previous lessons and activities, to assist them with maintaining goal directed behavior throughout the day

5. Students should always be able to articulate what their primary daily goals are at any time.

School Day Schedule		Done
(7:50 - 8:00)	*Ready for the day routine	☐
(8:05 - 8:50)	Algebra	☐
(8:55 - 9:40)	History	☐
(9:45 -10:30)	Tutorial/break	☐
(10:35 -11:20)	Biology	☐
(11:25 -12:05)	Lunch	☐
(12:10 -1:45)	Computer Science	☐
(1:50 - 2:35)	P.E.	☐
(2:35 - 2:45)	*Ready to go home routine	☐
(2:45)	Catch the bus	☐
Reviewed By:	☐	

Figure 5.6. Sample Daily School Schedule for a high school student. Note that the subjects may be COLOR coded to coordinate with the folders and book covers for those subjects.

Lesson 3-Activity 3: *Using a Calendar to Plot Short and Long Term Goals*

Materials

- GOALS WORKSHEET (ROPES 14)
- DECISION MATRIX FOR PRIORITIZATION (ROPES 15)
- PRIORITIES LADDER (ROPES 16)
- MONTHLY PLANNING CALENDAR (ROPES 08)
- HOMEWORK SUMMARY PAGE (ROPES 06-07)

Set Up

During the first planning session of the *month* have the students start by filling out the monthly GOALS WORKSHEET with all of the tasks, activities, assignments, etc. that they would like to complete or need to complete during that month. This Should Be A Regular Routine for the Class. These do not need to be in order at this point. Do not criticize or evaluate the items the student puts on the monthly GOALS WORKSHEET. For example, if a student wants to put, "Beat brother's high score on Grand Theft Auto" on his list, that would be acceptable. Students should also review the PRIORITIES LADDER in order to identify goals that need to be plotted on the MONTHLY PLANNING CALENDAR.

Plotting involves scheduling out the due dates and work time required for complex or multi-component tasks. When the students have identified and ranked their goals and priorities for the month this information may be plotted and adjusted as needed.

Steps for Participation

1. The students should review their HOMEWORK SUMMARY PAGE, the PRIORITIES LADDERS, GOAL WORKSHEETS, reminder boards, as well as the previous month's list of goals that were not completed.

2. Once the students have filled out the GOALS WORKSHEET, they should evaluate the items so they can be put in the DECISION MATRIX FOR PRIORITIZATION and subsequently be put in sequential order on a PRIORITIES LADDER.

3. Next have the students plot the activities in the MONTHLY PLANNING CALENDAR. The calendar should be evaluated and updated on a consistent schedule such as every Monday or Every Friday or the First Monday of the month.

4. If there are conflicting items the student will need to bump this item based on the DECISION MATRIX FOR PRIORITIZATION.

   a. If an item is bumped to a low priority it may be place on the reminder board for the next month.

Unit 6: Project Management

Objectives

- Students will learn to organize a long term project using organizational tools including graphic organizers, binders, folders, checklists, and calendars.
- Students will learn to organize an individual project using organizational tools including graphic organizers, binders, folders, checklists, and calendars.

Content for Teachers

Nothing necessitates the use of organization and planning skills more than the completion of a project. As parents of most students recognize, the first few projects that students are asked to do require a great deal of support. Teachers often break the project down into phases. The parent provides external support by procuring necessary materials, completion of each phase, and transporting the final product making sure it gets turned in on time without getting destroyed.

The difference in progression between a typical student and a student who struggles with EF is that the support can be faded after the first couple of projects as the student learns and generalizes the sequence of steps learned in the initial projects to new and novel projects that are assigned over the years. This is typically not the case for students with impaired EF. Students may freeze with inaction when presented with long term assignments or projects. Many do not know how to break the project down into chunks or how to monitor their progress toward completion. What we see then is what appears to be procrastination, waiting until the last minute and then scrambling to get it done, often with substantial support from well-meaning teachers and/or parents. This support certainly prevents failing the class or receiving zero credit, but ultimately does not help to further develop the EF Skills required for independent project management.

In this unit, we will break down the process of project management and teach the steps sequentially, first applying them to low stakes and fun projects and then assisting the students with generalization of these steps to school projects and higher stakes assignments.

| Unit 6: Lesson 1 | <u>Lesson 1</u>: **Planning and Implementing a Group Project** |

Materials

- BASIC CRITICAL THINKING SKILLS WORKSHEET (ROPES-13). Also referred to as CST "Thinking Tool"
- T CHARTS
- CLUSTER ORGANIZERS (ROPES-01, 02, 03).
- ORGANIZATION AND PLANNING WORKSHEETS (ROPES-12)
- ACTION PLANNING CARDS (ROPES-21)
- To do lists
- CHECKLIST (ROPES 05-05, 05-10, 05-15)
- MONTHLY PLANNING CALENDAR (ROPES-08)
- Project binder or folder with tabs
- Self Evaluation Rubric

Lesson 1-Activity 1: *Brainstorming Project Ideas*

Steps for Participation

1. Define for the student what is meant by a "project". According to Webster, 2016 a project is defined as: a planned piece of work that has a specific purpose, such as to find information or to make something new, and that usually requires a lot of time: a task or problem in school that requires careful work over a long period of time.

2. Explain to students that being able to manage projects is an important part of being a good student, but is also necessary in most jobs/professions.

3. Ask students to generate examples of projects that they have been assigned as students.

4. Ask students to generate examples of projects that are part of different jobs and professions.

5. Explain that this unit will be all about learning the skills and strategies to manage projects.

6. Ask the class to brainstorm a whole class group project they would like to work on for the next 3-4 weeks.

    a. Some examples could be: a canned food drive, a fund-raiser, planning and taking a field trip, planning and throwing a surprise party, planning and hosting a school wide movie night, making a skit or public service announcement, organizing an open house or parent night, hosting a peer party during lunch, etc.

7. Use a CLUSTER ORGANIZER to "brainstorm" the various ideas on the white board.

   a. In the center circle write "Project Ideas"

   b. In the outer circles write the student ideas as they are generated.

   c. List up to five ideas. Be sure that there are at least two realistic ideas that can be carried out within the time frame.

Lesson 1-Activity 2: *Evaluate Project Ideas*

Steps for Participation:

1. Ask students which of the graphic organizers that they have been working with would be a good tool for evaluating the ideas they have generated

   a. Prompt them to talk about each one.

2. Next complete a CST "Thinking Tool" organizer on each idea.

   a. In the circle write "Identify and carryout a class-wide project within the coming four weeks"

   b. In the squares write the choices or ideas to be evaluated

      i. Five ideas that were generated by the class

   c. The triangle is the intended goal or outcome of each project

   d. Have students discuss the pros and cons of each of the five choices using a T CHART.

3. Have students vote on the project ideas using the information gathered through the evaluation process.

   a. Emphasize to the students that they used a problem solving process that included looking at goals and outcomes of each project as well as pros and cons of each project.

   b. The idea with the most votes wins and is the class-wide project that the students will be working on for the next four weeks.

4. Post the CST "Thinking Tool" for the chosen project in the classroom somewhere as a reminder of the goal for the project.

Lesson 1-Activity 3: *Chunking the Project*

Steps for Participation

1. Inform the students that the project they have selected has many parts and components that need to be thought about and planned out.

   a. Ask the students which of the graphic organizers that they have been using and learning about is the best one for breaking things down or "chunking"

2. Guide the students to use either the CLUSTER ORGANIZER or the T CHART

3. If they select the CLUSTER ORGANIZER proceed as follows:

   a. In the center circle write the chosen idea.

   b. In the outer circles brainstorm the chunks and materials the students will need to plan and consider when organizing the event.

   c. Use extension circles to further define each of the outer circles.

      i. Extension circles could include people to contact, materials, resources, etc.

4. If they select the T CHART proceed as follows:

   a. Label the T CHART at the top with the project name.

   b. On the left side indicate the chunks or parts of the project that need to be planned for in order to organize the event.

   c. On the right side, break down the details for each chunk including the people to contact, materials, resources, etc.

Lesson 1-Activity 4: *Prioritizing Chunks*

Steps for Participation

1. Discuss each outer circle or chunk and prioritize each based on what needs to happen first, second, third, etc.

2. Put the tasks in order of priority on a TO DO LIST or a CHECKLIST with check off column.

3. Discuss and decide if students want to break into small groups to accomplish the items on the To Do lists or work on them together as a whole class.

   a. In addition, discuss students' strengths and interest areas as specific tasks are assigned.

4. Use a PLANNING CALENDAR to plug in the due date for the entire project, four weeks from start date, and benchmarks or cut points for the chunks of the project.

   a. Have students also estimate and plug in "work time" for each chunk.

Lesson 1-Activity 5: *Creating Action Plans and To-do Lists*

Steps for Participation

1. Set up a Project Binder with labeled Tabs.

2. Organize each chunk in the Project Binder with tab dividers labeled to represent each major chunk or task that is to be completed.

   a. Behind each tab, keep the to-do lists, action plans and any other information acquired to complete that step or component of the project.

   b. Create an "Action Plan" for each chunk which includes materials needed, people responsible, due dates and steps.

   c. Use ACTION PLANNING CARDS and ORGANIZATION AND PLANNING WORKSHEETS as needed to assist with implementing plans for task completion.

3. Place the Planning Calendar in the front of the binder with due dates highlighted.

4. The teacher should keep the Master Project Binder in class for the students to use and access each day.

   a. The project binder process will be the same process they will use when completing individual projects and assignments (e.g., science projects, research papers, etc.).

Stress to students the organized and systematic order in which each component of this group project will be similar to how they would complete an assignment given by their teachers in other classes.

Lesson 1-Activity 6: *Execute the Plan and Self-Monitor Progress*

Steps for Participation

1. Have students begin to work on their project using their action plans, checklists, etc.

   a. Check in with them daily to see if their plans are working, need to be revised, added to or rethought.

2. Have students self-evaluate how they are doing at the end of each class period.

   a. This can be done using a daily *Self-Assessment* or a *Project Management Rubric* created by the class.

3. At each benchmark date or cut point that was identified on the planning calendar have the students report back on progress to the entire group.

   a. Have students revise their timeline on the planning calendar as needed.

4. After the project is completed, have the students evaluate their goal.

   a. Have them evaluate whether they met the goal or did not by referring to the CST "Thinking Tool".

5. Use a T CHART and lead a discussion about "Things that went well" and "Things that did not go well."

   a. Ask them to identify things they would do differently if they did the project again.

| Unit 6: Lesson 2 | **Lesson 2: Planning and Implementing an Individual Project** |

Steps for Participation

1. Now, repeat the process described above on an individual student basis

2. Post a Steps for Project Management poster for class reference:

   a. Brainstorm project ideas

   b. Evaluate ideas

   c. Select project

   d. Identify project components/chunks

   e. Set timelines and checkpoints

   f. Develop and use checklists

   g. Evaluate progress

   h. Refine plans as needed

3. These steps are critical components of learning to manage a long term project.

4. Students can use actual school projects assigned in other core classes or the teacher can work with them on identifying projects that are for relevant in the current class.

    a. Examples of a project topics might include:

        i. Learning about their disability

        ii. Famous people who have disabilities

        iii. Conducting a research project on various jobs or professions of interest to them

5. If students want to work on a project from a core class, the core teachers should be contacted to identify upcoming projects that will be assigned in those classes.

    a. With this information, support for the students can begin immediately as they start work on the assignment.

    b. For example, if students have an upcoming project for History, the Study Skills teacher can get project details from the History teacher and provide support and structure within the class to assist the students in completing the History Project.

    c. Study Skills teachers may need to work with core teachers on modifications and/or alternative due dates. It may also be helpful to conduct collaborative grading so that the student receives point for "process" as well as the final product.

Notes:

Unit 7: Self-Awareness, Self-Monitoring and Self-Management

Objectives

- Students will become aware of their strengths and weaknesses and learn to advocate for assistance when needed.

- Students will learn to use supports to improve their ability to self-evaluate, monitor and manage their reactions and behaviors in a variety of situations.

- Students will learn to use external visual supports and graphic organizers to improve their ability to self-manage stress and frustration in a variety of situations.

- Students will learn to Self Advocate and request needed assistance and resources across various situations to assist them in coping with challenges and obstacles.

Content for Teachers

In order for students to change any behavior or habit, they must first be aware of when they are engaged in the behavior. Once the students have developed awareness they will be ready to self-monitor and manage themselves.

Self-monitoring, also referred to as self-recording, self-observation, and self-evaluation, involves the students observing and recording the occurrence or non-occurrence of their own behavior. This is a useful tool for teaching self-management because it is necessary for people to accurately measure their own behavior in order to determine if that behavior is changing in the desired direction.

Self-management is a technique that facilitates independence by systematically fading reliance on external praise and shifts control to the student (Smith, L. and fowler, S. 1984). Research has shown that when self-management of specific target behaviors is taught there is also a significant decrease in other maladaptive behaviors that have not been targeted for intervention (Koegel, L., Koegel, R., Hurley, C, and Frea, W. 1982). Teaching self-management will decrease the need for on-going support and assistance that can limit students' ability to become self-sufficient. Developing these skills will have lifelong implications as the students transition to future education, employment, and relationships.

Unit 7: Lesson 1 | <u>**Lesson 1:** Increasing Self-Awareness</u>

Materials

- SELF EVALUATION STRESS TRIGGERS (ROPES 25)
- SELF EVALUATION EFFICIENCY (ROPES 26)
- EFQ SELF EVALUATION

Set Up

Explain that in order to change an undesirable behavior it is important to have an accurate idea of strengths and weaknesses. These will become the foundation for identifying new skills and behaviors that students may want to learn.

Lesson 1-Acitivty 1: *Determining, Sharing, and Summarizing Strengths and Weaknesses*

1. Have students complete the EFQ SELF EVALUATION
   a. Students may need some assistance to accurately complete the forms.
   b. Optional: This could be assigned as homework so that family members may be able to help students think about real life scenarios.
2. Once the forms are completed have the students identify to following:
   a. Three (3) areas of strength
   b. Three (3) areas of weakness or areas for improvement
3. Have the students share these with their peers in a small group setting
4. Have the small group summarize all their strengths and weaknesses
   a. Have the small group present them to the whole group
5. This practice will assist students in learning several skills including:
   a. How to articulate their strengths and weaknesses
   b. Taking perspective of others
   c. Learning that they may share similarities with others

Lesson 1-Activity 2: *Self-Monitoring On and Off Task Behaviors*

Materials

- Timer
- T CHARTS

Steps for Participation

1. Draw a T CHART on the board and label the left side as "On Task/Working" and the right side as "Off Task/Not Working".

2. Have students describe in detail what "On Task/Working" looks like.

3. The target behavior should be defined specifically and in concrete measurable terms. For example:

    a. Looking at materials

    b. Talking about materials/task

    c. Completing the task

    d. Asking questions about the task

    e. Making comments about the task

    f. Staying in seat

4. Then have the students describe what "Off Task/Not Working" looks like. For example:

    a. Walking around the room

    b. Talking about other topics

    c. Looking away from teacher and materials

    d. Turning away from the group or materials

    e. Looking at other students

    f. Asking off topic questions

    NOTE: These behavioral descriptions should be kept on the board for the following activity and for easy reference during the school year.

5. Next, have students make their own T CHART with "On Task" of the left side and "Off Task" on the right side.

6. Have each student develop a "work plan" for the remainder of the period that includes specific homework or schoolwork activities that must be completed.

    a. If students don't have work, create some simple tasks, assignments or silent reading.

    b. Ideally these activities will be solitary activities since group activities may be more difficult to determine reliability.

7. Next, explain to the students that they will be "self-monitoring" their own On Task and Off Task behaviors for the remainder of the class and for a portion of subsequent classes.

8. The teacher should set a timer and ask the students to "get to work".

   a. The timer should be set for variable intervals of time ranging from 1 minute to 15 minutes.

9. When the timer sounds, the students should stop what they are doing and self-evaluate whether they were On or Off Task using the predetermined definition that was created earlier.

10. Students should put a tally in the appropriate side of the T CHART based on the behavior they were doing when the timer rang.

    a. For the first few sessions, the teacher should call on students and ask them to tell the group how they scored themselves, on-task verses off-task, and why.

    b. Rewards should be given for accurately identifying their own behaviors.

    c. If they were "off-task", but they clearly indicated and described that they were "off-task" they should receive points.

    d. The goal is accuracy of self-recording at this point, "not on task behavior" itself.

11. Inter-Observer Reliability Checks: Teach this process after 15-20 minutes of practice depending on how quickly students acquire the concept of self-monitoring.

    a. Reliability Checks for self-monitoring "On and Off Task" behaviors can be accomplished by having the students self-monitor their behavior for a preset period of time while a partner (i.e., teacher, assistant or peer) also measures the same behavior.

    b. At the end of the interval of time the student and partner should compare the T CHARTS to determine if they agreed upon the number of occurrences of "On or Off" tasks behaviors.

    c. The teacher may need to select only a few students each day to conduct reliability checks on, or enlist the help of teaching assistants or peers.

12. To determine reliability or inter-observer agreement, the students and their partners should divide the number of instances in which they agreed on the occurrence of

the On Tasks Behaviors by the total number of instances (agreements plus disagreements).

13. NOTE: The goal is 80% agreement, which can be easily calculated using the following formula:

Agreements_____x 100 =_____Percent of Agreements

_____

Agreements + Disagreements

Figure 7.1 Calculation Format for Inter-Observer Agreement

14. Initially the students' accuracy in self-monitoring should be heavily rewarded with positive feedback and possibly some additional tangible rewards or points.

15. Continue this process until each student has reliable inter-observer agreement of at least 80%.

16. Reliability of self-monitoring is said to be established when there is 80% or better inter-observer agreement for three consecutive measurement sessions as noted by Barlow, D., and Hersen, M., (1976).

Lesson 1-Activity 3: *Increasing On Task Time in Class*

Set Up

Explain to students that getting a baseline allows them to know the current rate or frequency of the behavior.

Steps for Participation

1. Once students reach 80% inter-observer agreement with a partner, then go through the process of setting goals to increase the amount of time spent On Task.

2. Goals should be set to increase On Task time by 10-20% at a time to make success obtainable.

3. If On Task time is only 50% then the goal should be set at 60% On Task time.

   a. Increase the goal by reasonable and obtainable increments.

The Study Skills Curriculum

Unit 7: Lesson 2 **Lesson 2:** Self-Managing Undesired or Problematic Behaviors

Lesson 2-Activity 1: *Selecting a Behavior to Change and Collecting Baseline*

Materials

- COMPLETED EFQ SELF EVALUATIONAL
- Previous quarter's grades
- T CHART
- SELF-IMPROVEMENT CONTRACT (ROPES 24)

Set Up

The teacher may identify a behavior to change with the group prior to having the students do the activity in small groups or individually. Some students may have limited behavioral self awareness. In these cases the teacher might get suggestions for behavioral change from the students' parents or other teachers.

Steps for Participation

1. Have the students review their EFQ SELF EVALUATION and have them identify a target behavior they want to change. The target behavior can be any behavior that is important to the student.

2. Record the target behavior on the left side of a T CHART.

3. On the right side have the students describe an alternative appropriate response or replacement behavior they would like to or should do instead.

4. Example: Target behaviors could be from their EFQ SELF EVALUATIONAL or something different such as biting fingernails, interrupting people who are talking, turning in homework for math, being rigid and inflexible, etc. Students will require assistance in clearly and specifically defining the behavior they have targeted to change.

5. Next have the students identify the method for measuring that behavior and the time interval they will use to self-record.

   a. Methods include time intervals which track how long the target behavior occurs or lasts or frequency of occurrence of the target behavior within a preset period.

110

   b. Next have the students record their behavior for a preset amount of time such as one, two or three day periods of time, to get the current rate of the behavior they are targeting for change.

6. It should be noted that this is not a true "baseline" since research reveals that the act of measuring your own behavior does change your behavior. The real purpose of this "baseline" period is to assist the students with setting a goal for earning the predetermined reward.

Lesson 2-Activity 2: *Using Self-Improvement Contracts to Change a Target Behavior*

Set up

To facilitate the development and implementation of self-management plans, it is helpful to utilize the SELF-IMPROVEMENT CONTRACT. This contract can be used to work on decreasing problematic behaviors, such as calling out in class, as well as improving other skills and behaviors, such as completing a morning hygiene routine. The chosen behavior should be meaningful and individualized to each student. This may take some time to help students choose the behavior to change.

Materials

- SELF-IMPROVEMENT CONTRACT (ROPES 24)

Steps for Participation:

1. The teacher should introduce the SELF-IMPROVEMENT CONTRACT to the students and explain that it is a tool used to allow the students to learn to manage their own behaviors.

2. Initially staff may need to assist the students in completing the contract. However, the students should begin to fill out the contract independently with decreasing feedback, and eventually with total independence over the course of the school year as new behaviors are identified for change. It may be beneficial to complete a sample with the whole class using the board to demonstrate the process.

3. As indicated on the SELF-IMPROVEMENT CONTRACT, the students must first identify the target behavior. This can be a behavior they would like to improve or increase, such

as completing a hygiene routine, or a behavior they would like to decrease, such as calling out in class. This step may have been accomplished during the self-monitoring procedure.

4. The next thing the students must do is assess their own motivation for changing the behavior. Once they have identified the rationale for changing the behavior, they can write it on the contract. This may include both natural and arbitrary outcomes. Students must identify an appropriate replacement behavior in order for the plan to be effective. For example, if calling out answers is the target behavior then a replacement behavior could be to write the answers down in a notebook or on a post-it note. Another replacement behavior could be "wait to be called on." This step must not be skipped. It will be critical to help students to identify replacement behaviors and practice them regularly.

5. A measurable goal should be determined and written on the contract. The goal should include the replacement behavior that will increase and the target behavior that will decrease. This is essentially the criterion for earning the reinforcer or experiencing a consequence for not meeting the criteria outlined. It is usually best to set the criterion level for *no more than 50* % of the baseline, initially. The baseline was established in the previous activity using the self-monitoring procedure described earlier in this unit.

6. The criterion should be systematically changed as improvement is shown. For example, if the goal is for the students to independently complete a morning hygiene routine and the baseline was only two days out of five, the initial goal might be three days out of five. If the goal was to decrease talking out while increasing hand raising and the baseline was five times per hour talking out and one time per hour hand-raising, a good criterion to start with might be three times per hour or less for talking out and two times per hour or more for hand raising.

NOTE: The criterion for behavior change should be adjusted according to each student's success. If the students are successfully reaching criterion levels for a few days, then increase the expectations. If the students are not meeting criterion, it may be necessary to either decrease the expectation, reassess the reinforcers, or make sure that the students fully understand and know how to *do* the identified behavior (e.g., make sure they know how to complete all of the steps of the morning hygiene routine).

7. Once the criterion is set, then the process for self-monitoring the behavior should resume. It should also indicate how or if another person will assist with reliability checks. These pieces of the plan should be specified on the contract.

8. Finally, a review and evaluation process needs to be determined. This should be indicated on the SELF-IMPROVEMENT CONTRACT.

9. For independent self-management, the students should be responsible for measuring the behavior without requiring ongoing reliability checks and initiating the reinforcer if arbitrary rewards are necessary. For example, if the student meets criterion for the predetermined number of days, then the student would go to the teacher or another designated person to show the data and ask for the reward.

10. Eventually the students will self-administer the reward once the criterion level is met. To do this, the reward should be accessible to the students without requiring an adult to get it. Periodic data checks should take place to insure that the students are continuing to accurately keep track of their target behaviors.

Figure 7.2 **SELF-IMPROVEMENT CONTRACT**

The behavior I want to change is:

The reason I want to change the behavior is:

My replacement behavior is:

My Measurable Goal is:

If I meet the goal then:

If I do not meet the goal then:

I will enlist the help of:

This person/device will help me by doing the following:

Lesson 3: Self-Management of Stress and Frustration

Lesson 3-Activity 1: *Managing Stress and Frustration*

Set up

Initially students may need to work on simply identifying feelings of frustration and/or stress. Once the students are successfully able to identify feelings of frustration and stress, they can work on strategies for evaluating and self-managing them. This can be done using the critical thinking skills model as structured in the SELF-EVALUATION OF STRESS TRIGGERS WORKSHEET.

Materials

- BASIC CRITICAL THINKING SKILLS WORKSHEET (ROPES-13). Also referred to as CST "Thinking Tool"
- SELF EVALUATION OF STRESS TRIGGERS WORKSHEET (ROPES 25)
- Create 10-15 scenarios that occur naturally such as traffic, forgot an appointment, too much work to complete, late to a meeting, meeting someone new, going to a new place, not being heard, being ignored etc.

Steps for Participation:

1. Draw the CST "Thinking Tool" on the board and show the students personal examples of managing stress or frustration.

2. Complete the SELF EVALUATION OF STRESS TRIGGERS WORKSHEET on the board as a model for the students.

   a. Follow the same process and assist each student in developing specific and individualized plans for their own stress triggers.

   b. Each student's plan will be unique.

   c. This process may take some time.

3. As the students identify situations that result in feelings of frustration and/or stress, have them write in the circle labeled "Triggers."

4. Then have the students identify all of the current ways they react or respond to these stress triggers.

   a. Have students write their answers in the square labeled "Responses."

5. Next have the students list what happens as a result of their current methods of reacting in the triangle labeled Outcomes.

    a. Discuss how situations cause responses and responses have outcomes referring to the CST "Thinking Tool" strategy.

    b. Help them to see the connection and relationship between these elements. This information should be recorded on the SELF-EVALUATION OF STRESS TRIGGERS WORKSHEET.

6. Ask students to identify possible ways of handling the stress triggers when they are faced with them, write them in a new square labeled "New Reactions."

    a. This might include things like social scripts, self-talk scripts, deep breathing/relaxation routines, help seeking routines, drawing, journaling etc.

7. The ACTION PLAN for dealing with these stressors should be indicated on the SELF EVALUATION OF STRESS TRIGGERS WORKSHEET.

8. Have the students determine and predict the likely outcomes of learning and using these coping strategies, rather than their previous responses and choices.

    a. The predicted outcomes should be recorded in a new triangle on their SELF EVALUATION OF STRESS TRIGGERS WORKSHEET.

    b. This will show the students the long-term and natural rewards that these alternative responses will produce.

9. Next have the students identify ways of preventing exposure to the stress triggers.

    a. This might include things like sitting in a certain part of the room, wearing headphones to filter out certain unpleasant sounds, etc.

    b. These prevention strategies should be indicated on in a new circle on the worksheet.

10. In addition to preventing exposure, a plan for self-advocacy should be developed.

    a. In this plan, the students should learn to tell others in advance what situations are stressful for them and devise a proactive plan for preventing their occurrence and/or dealing with them when they arise.

    b. These prevention and self-advocacy plans should also be indicated on the SELF EVALUATION OF STRESS TRIGGERS WORKSHEET.

    c. For example, if the students know that working in groups creates high stress, they might devise a self-advocacy plan for telling new teachers about their need to work independently whenever possible.

11. Once the self-evaluation and planning process described above is complete, the students could develop and begin implementing a self-management plan for the identified stress prevention and coping strategies using the SELF-IMPROVEMENT CONTRACT.

12. This process should be ongoing and continually monitored and updated throughout the school year.

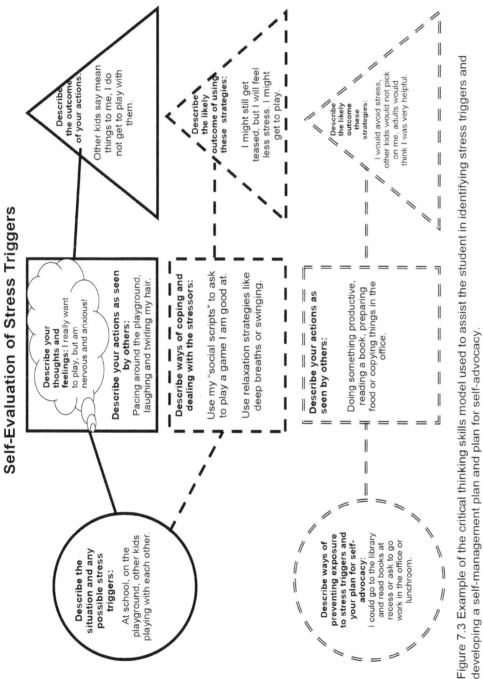

Self-Evaluation of Stress Triggers

Describe the outcome of your actions.
Other kids say mean things to me, I do not get to play with them.

Describe the likely outcome of using these strategies:
I might still get teased, but I will feel less stress. I might get to play.

Describe the likely outcome these strategies:
I would avoid stress, other kids would not pick on me, adults would think I was very helpful.

Describe your thoughts and feelings: I really want to play, but am nervous and anxious!

Describe your actions as seen by others:
Pacing around the playground, laughing and twirling my hair.

Describe ways of coping and dealing with the stressors:
Use my "social scripts" to ask to play a game I am good at.
Use relaxation strategies like deep breaths or swinging.

Describe your actions as seen by others:
Doing something productive, reading a book, preparing food or copying things in the office.

Describe the situation and any possible stress triggers:
At school, on the playground, other kids playing with each other.

Describe ways of preventing exposure to stress triggers and your plan for self-advocacy:
I could go to the library and read books at recess or ask to go work in the office or lunchroom.

Figure 7.3 Example of the critical thinking skills model used to assist the student in identifying stress triggers and developing a self-management plan and plan for self-advocacy.

Unit 7: Lesson 4 — Lesson 4: Self-Management of Efficiency

Materials

- TIME JOURNAL (ROPES 10)
- SELF EVALUATION EFFICIENCY (ROPES 26)
- SELF IMPROVEMENT CONTRACT (ROPES 24)

Lesson 4-Activity 1: *Improving Efficiency*

1. Have the students identify those tasks from the TIME JOURNAL that are taking longer than expected or longer than they would like.

2. Next have the students work on completing the SELF EVALUATION EFFICIENCY worksheet by first identifying any competing behaviors and distractions that were in the environment while they were trying to complete these specific tasks (e.g., what were they doing or attending to instead of the task at hand).

   a. Responses can be written on the board if you are providing a whole group example and on the SELF EVALUATION OF EFFICIENCY worksheet.

3. Next have the students identify ways of preventing these distractions.

   a. Make a plan for eliminating the temptation to engage in the competing behavior and rearranging the environment so that the potential distractions are decreased or eliminated. Help students to develop a specific and meaningful plan.

   b. Record responses on the board and have students write these on the SELF EVALUATION EFFICIENCY worksheet.

4. Finally have the students identify ways of increasing motivation to complete tasks in a timely manner.

   a. This can include evaluating the natural outcomes of being more efficient which leads to having more time for preferred activities or free time or implementing some type of motivational system for increasing efficiency.

   b. The students should write this information on the SELF EVALUATION EFFICIENCY worksheet.

5. Once this evaluation process is complete, the students could develop a written self-management plan for improving efficiency utilizing the SELF-IMPROVEMENT CONTRACT.

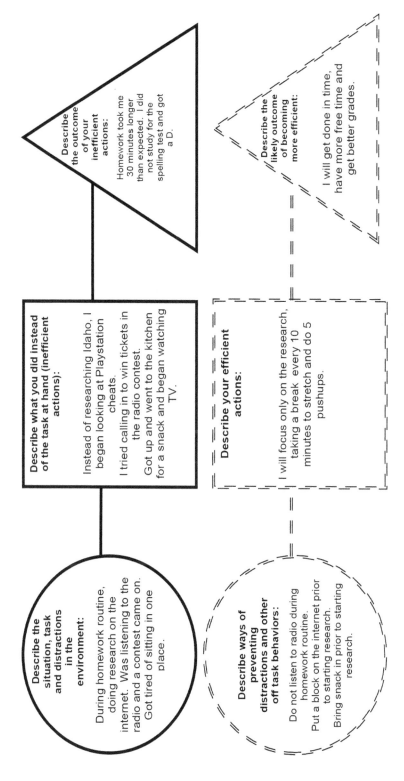

Self-Evaluation of Efficiency

Describe the situation, task and distractions in the environment:

During homework routine, doing research on the internet. Was listening to the radio and a contest came on. Got tired of sitting in one place.

Describe what you did instead of the task at hand (inefficient actions):

Instead of researching Idaho, I began looking at Playstation cheats.
I tried calling in to win tickets in the radio contest.
Got up and went to the kitchen for a snack and began watching TV.

Describe the outcome of your inefficient actions:

Homework took me 30 minutes longer than expected. I did not study for the spelling test and got a D.

Describe ways of preventing distractions and other off task behaviors:

Do not listen to radio during homework routine.
Put a block on the internet prior to starting research.
Bring snack in prior to starting research.

Describe your efficient actions:

I will focus only on the research, taking a break every 10 minutes to stretch and do 5 pushups.

Describe the likely outcome of becoming more efficient:

I will get done in time, have more free time and get better grades.

Figure 7.4 Example of the critical thinking skills model used for assisting the student at evaluating and developing an action plan to improve his/her rate of efficiency with tasks.

119

Unit 7: Lesson 5 — Lesson 5: Self-Advocacy

Set Up

It is essential that students learn to recognize and advocate for the supports and assistance they need. They must learn about their needs so they can improve their ability to function in various settings and develop coping skills. The most important skill that any student can learn is how to request assistance and support from others when it is necessary. This is called "Self-Advocacy." Students with disabilities need to learn how to self-disclose information about their disability and the resulting reasonable accommodations that they need to do a job or be a successful student. This is especially critical as students prepare for college and will need to speak up for themselves. The ability to self-advocate can only be accomplished through self-awareness and practice. Students need to learn to practice telling others, in a constructive way, what is hard for them and what others can do to help. In addition, it is critical that students learn how to accept feedback as they will need to do this in many life situations including work.

As you go through the activities for Self-Advocacy in this section, it may be useful to complete some examples as a group. Explain to students that tasks can have easy and hard components but the critical part of completing the task is being able to identify strategies that will help with successfully completing it. This will usually include asking for assistance or resources. This activity helps students break tasks into columns and identify strategies that could help them be successful. Sometime students avoid difficult tasks or give up in the midst of them if they are not able to identify strategies to help them be successful.

Materials

- Develop a variety of real life situations to use as role play activities:
  - Ask for directions to a building
  - Locate a phone or office
  - Request a price of an object
  - Ask someone to repeat directions
  - Ask someone for more time
  - Request a break or help, etc.
  - Ask to leave a situation
  - These scenarios may be drawn from the students' self-evaluations or from their own accommodation plans that are part of their IEP/504 Plan.
- T CHARTS

Lesson 5-Activity 1: *Improving Self-Advocacy*

1. Draw a CHART on the board with three columns.

   a. Label the left column Easy Tasks,

   b. The middle column Hard Tasks

   c. The right column Strategies that Help.

2. Select a scenario and separate it into Easy and Hard Tasks on the T CHART.

3. In the third column on the T CHART ask students to offer ideas and suggestions for what could be helpful.

4. When students indicate that asking others for support can sometimes be helpful begin a discussion about the differences between *Help vs Criticism*

   a. You can use a T CHART to contrast these two different forms of feedback.

   b. Give students suggestions and strategies for reframing their thoughts about feedback. For example, if they feel like someone is criticizing them rather than helping:

      i. Cognitive Reframe 1: Some people are trying to help but maybe they are not very good at giving feedback.

      ii. Cognitive Reframe 2: Needing help is not a bad thing, it is a way to increase by abilities. This person may be able to assist me with increasing my skills.

      iii. Self-Advocacy: Stating to the other person that the feedback is critical rather than helpful and that it would be better if the feedback was more descriptive or detailed.

5. Have the students each create their own T CHARTS with things that are Easy/Hard and Helpful. This can be done by asking them to do it for each of their classes.

6. If students are comfortable, have them share their T CHARTS with a partner or the whole group.

7. In order to further develop Self Disclosure and Self Advocacy Skills, have the students present their charts at their IEP meetings or at a teacher conference with their core class teachers. Practicing this skill in the safe environment of a public school will further prepare them for college and the world of employment.

Table of Figures

Forms Index

INFORMATION HANDOUTS

<u>SAMPLE GOALS AND OBJECTIVES</u>

ROPES-SGO.pdf

FORMS TO PRINT AND FILL IN BY HAND

<u>COMPANION PACK WORKSHEETS</u>

ROPES-Forms.pdf
ROPES-01-ClusterOrganizer.pdf
ROPES-02-ClusterOrganizerRecall.pdf
ROPES-03-ClusterOrganizer02.pdf
ROPES-04-SequentialOrganizer.pdf
ROPES-05-05TaskChecklist.pdf
ROPES-05-10TaskChecklist.pdf
ROPES-05-15TaskChecklist.pdf
ROPES-06-HomeworkSummaryPage.pdf
ROPES-07-HomeworkSummaryPage.pdf
ROPES-08-MonthlyPlanningCalendar.pdf
ROPES-09-DailySchedule.pdf
ROPES-10-TimeJournal.pdf
ROPES-11-VennDiagramForComparingActivities.pdf
ROPES-12-OrganizationAndPlanningWorksheet.pdf
ROPES-13-BasicCriticalThinkingSkillsWorksheet.pdf
ROPES-14-GoalsWorksheet.pdf
ROPES-15-DecisionMatrixForPrioritization.pdf
ROPES-16-PrioritiesLadder.pdf
ROPES-17-EvaluatingAndResolvingProblematicBehavior.pdf
ROPES-18-19-BehaviorProblemSolving.pdf
ROPES-20-EvaluatingAndSelectingApproopriateActions.pdf
ROPES-21-ActionPlanCard.pdf
ROPES-22-EvaluationOfNovelSituations.pdf
ROPES-23-MonitorCharts.pdf
ROPES-24-SelfImprovementContract.pdf
ROPES-25-Self-EvaluationStressTriggers.pdf
ROPES-26-Self-EvaluationEfficiency.pdf

<u>EXECUTIVE FUNCTIONING QUESTIONNAIRES
AND SCORING PROCEDURES</u>

ROPES-EvaluationSet.pdf
ROPES-SelfEvaluation.pdf
ROPES-TeacherEvaluation.pdf
ROPES-ScoringProcedures.pdf

Forms Index Continued

BONUS FORMS Included.

Instructions for Downloading
R.O.P.E.S. SSC Forms

1. Open your favorite browser (Chrome, Safari, Firefox, Internet Explorer, etc.)

2. Type in the following address **24.205.237.234**

3. Press Return

4. When the login screen appears type in the information found at the bottom of this page

5. Click on the file(s) that you wish to download

6. When all downloads have been completed, please close your browser to log-off

7. If you have any difficulty with the downloads please seek help by sending an email to the address below

User Name: **ropesssc**
Password**: mh376cet4**
Any issues contact:
jpkingavpro@charter.net

CPSIA information can be obtained
at www.ICGtesting.com
Printed in the USA
BVHW011025160819
555732BV00014BA/360/P